Jewish Displaced Persons
in Camp Bergen-Belsen 1945-1950

THEY RETURNED

WITH PRIDE

DAISM

JOY.

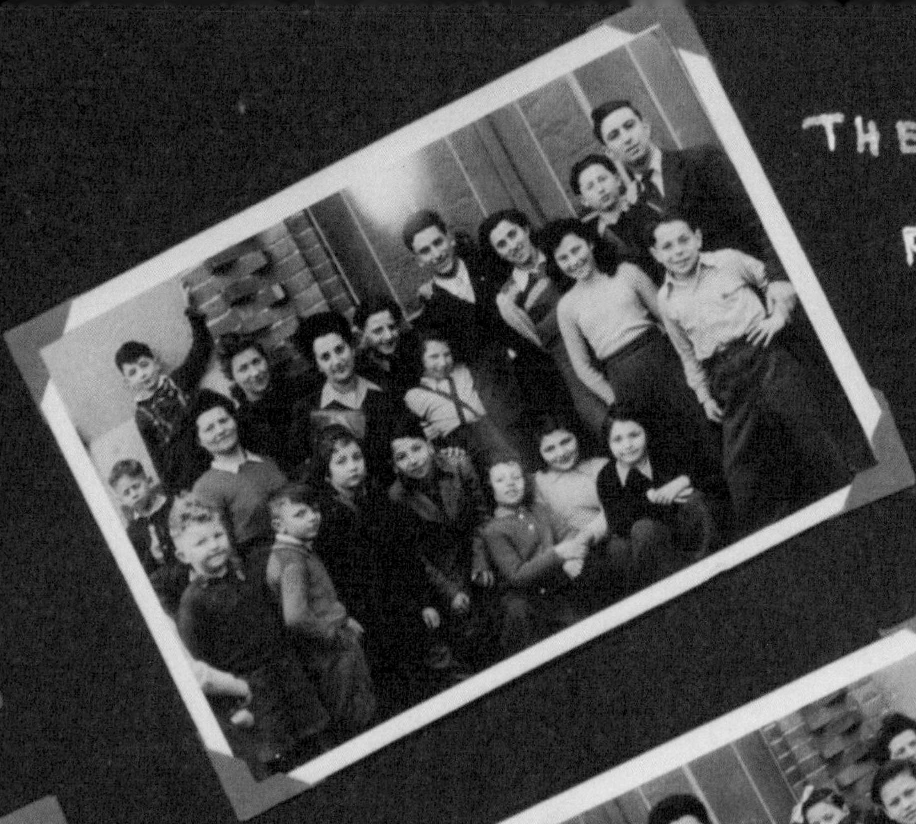

THE CHIL
FELT T
MIGH
BE
IN

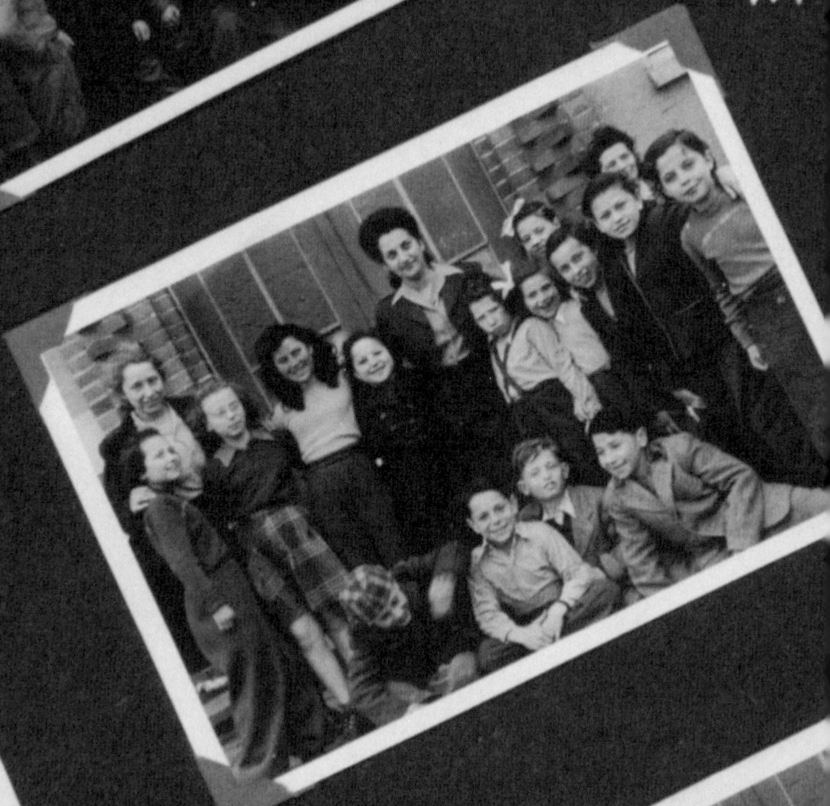

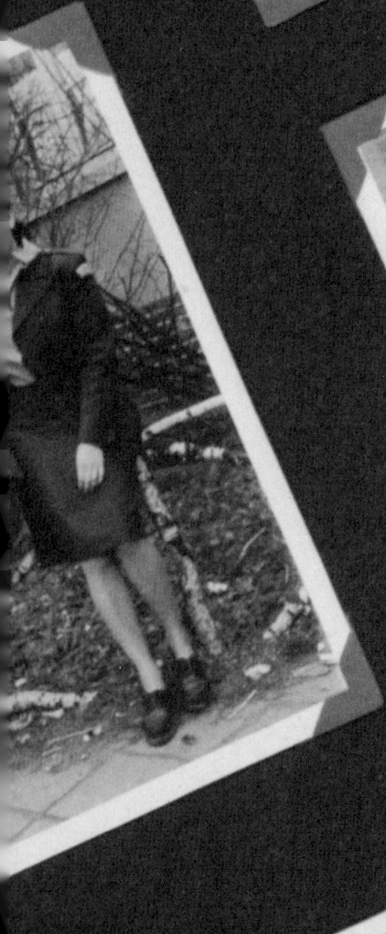

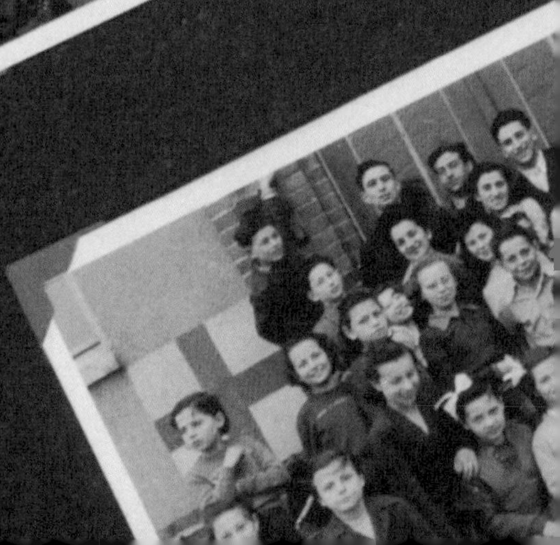

NOW

AVE

RE

ND THE DAY

WAS

SPENT

IN

TAKING

PICTURES:

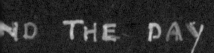

Dedicated to the memory of Eric Nooter

Jewish Displaced Persons in Camp Bergen-Belsen
1945-1950

The Unique Photo Album of Zippy Orlin

Edited by Erik Somers and René Kok

A Samuel and Althea Stroum Book

University of Washington Press
Seattle
in association with
Netherlands Institute for War Documentation

Contents

Introduction

Erik Somers en René Kok

On September 19, 1986 Chaim Orlin, age 51, visited the Netherlands Institute for War Documentation (NIOD) at its stately premises overlooking one of the old canals of Amsterdam. A portly man, Chaim was visibly exhausted from lugging a large, heavy photograph album. He explained that he had intended to entrust this photograph collection to a historic archive for a long time. Since Chaim lived in Amsterdam, he considered the Netherlands Institute for War Documentation to be the most appropriate place. After all, this institute is internationally renowned for its vast collection of archives and photographs about World War II and the aftermath of this turbulent period. Chaim Orlin felt a sense of urgency. In his rush, he shared few details upon handing over the impressive 33-pound album. He merely explained that his sister Cecillia "Zippy" Orlin had composed the album from photographs taken during the period when the former concentration camp Bergen-Belsen was used as a DP camp for Jewish survivors of the Nazi atrocities. With that, Chaim Orlin hurriedly left the canal premises.

Initial examination revealed the immense historical value of the album. Containing over one thousand photographs, it provides a detailed reflection of the Displaced Persons camp Bergen-Belsen. The scenes raise several questions. Who was Zippy Orlin, had she taken all the photographs, how had the document ended up in the Netherlands? Chaim Orlin would know. Four days after receiving the album, we contacted the donor. To our dismay, we learned that Chaim had died in his sleep the night before.

The Bergen-Belsen album was added to the photograph collection of the Netherlands Institute of War Documentation with a brief description. Years later the opportunity arose to investigate the album in detail. Altogether, there are 1,117 photographs with brief captions affixed to 112 pages of an old-fashioned photo album with end leaves. Most of the photographs are amateur snapshots, except for forty photographs made by the press photographer Ursula Litzmann. They convey many aspects of life at the Displaced Persons camp Bergen-Belsen. We published our findings and a selection of the photographs in the 1998 Yearbook of the Netherlands Institute for War Documentation.[1] An abridged English translation of the article appears on the website.[2]

The article and especially the photographs have received extensive media coverage. The most authoritative news bulletin in the Netherlands opened on prime time with the announcement that a remarkable photograph collection had been rescued from oblivion. Israeli television and a few local television stations in the United States featured the item. Soon afterwards, we decided to compose a book about the album.

In the article we wrote that Zippy Orlin, who assembled the contents of the album, had been a volunteer for the American Jewish Joint Distribution Committee (AJDC) at the DP camp Bergen-Belsen. Eric Nooter, archivist for the AJDC in New York, contacted the NIOD following the first publicity about the photo collection. Born in the Netherlands, Eric Nooter traveled from New York to Amsterdam to examine the photographs in detail.[3] At the congress *Life Reborn. Jewish Displaced Persons 1945-1951* held in Washington, D.C., in January 2000, Eric Nooter presented a selection of photographs from the album.[4] His audience included Holocaust survivors who had spent brief or extended periods as DPs at the camp. His expertise and enthusiasm about the subject were very inspiring. Eric was already seriously ill at the time and thus unable to contribute his article to this book. Sections of his draft text have been added to the article that Sara Kadosh contributed to this book. Erik Nooter died on August 3, 2000. This book is dedicated to him.

The history of the Bergen-Belsen camp includes two extremes: death and survival. During the final months that Bergen-Belsen was used as a concentration camp under the Nazis, it was plagued by death. Tens of thousands of prisoners succumbed to utter exhaustion and the epidemics that ravaged the camp. A survivor described the camp as follows: "Perhaps fewer people died than at Birkenau, but death was more visible. At Birkenau entire groups disappeared ... If they wrote down your name at Birkenau, your time was up. Death was very efficient and neat there. At Bergen-Belsen nobody said goodbye, people died slowly from disease, exhaustion, cold, mostly from starvation ... At Bergen-Belsen death lurked everywhere."[5] Upon liberating the camp in the midst of a typhus epidemic on April 15, 1945, British troops found over 60,000 emaciated, desperate survivors of various nationalities. They included many Jews, some political prisoners and a few Sinti and Roma prisoners.

The Photo Album of Zippy Orlin, comprising 112 pages with flyleaves and containing 1,117 photographs. Dimensions: 24" x 17", weight: 33 lbs.

Upon the liberation, the history of Bergen-Belsen changed from a tale of victims to one of survivors. Until 1950, Bergen-Belsen, which was in the British Zone of Occupation in Germany, was one of Europe's largest internally autonomous communities of Holocaust survivors. Refugees fleeing the post-war surge of virulent anti-Semitism in Eastern Europe soon settled there. Displaced Persons built a new life in the camp while trying to find a new home-land as well. An individual, autonomous society emerged at the camp, comprising schools, medical facilities, a police force, a court of law, a news service and cultural and religious activities. The main objective of the Jewish leaders and some of the organizations helping the DPs was to reinforce Jewish identity and foster Zionist sentiment, which was encouraged by the international debate surrounding the establishment of the Jewish State of Israel. Historian Hagit Lavsky has described this process as follows: "Life in the camp was a green-house for a new Jewish identity."[6]

The album of Zippy Orlin features illustrative and often compelling scenes depicting the tentative efforts of the survivors to recover and resume normal lives after the horrors of the Holocaust. This book is about the photographs in the album and addresses them by theme. The scenes reveal all aspects of everyday life, from leisure, education and work through weddings and the care of the many orphans. Volunteer Zippy Orlin was primarily responsible for the very youngest children. The camp administration and the counselors wanted the children to have faith and look forward to a different, better future. Zippy's caption to one of the photographs from the album of Barrack RB 7 (the kinder-garten) was: "The Children of rb7 were molded into one big happy family and learned to laugh and play again."

The camp population longed to immigrate to Israel, the nascent Jewish state, more than anything else in the world. In the album are photographs of the few transports of DPs authorized by the Allies in 1947. These transports included many Jewish children. Escorted by AJDC staff, they departed for Palestine. The first chapter reviews the background to the album and of Zippy Orlin, the woman who compiled it.

The German researchers Angelika Königseder and Juliane Wetzel have outlined the problems of Displaced Persons in the British sector of post-war Germany and focus primarily on the political aspects of DP issues. With over 10,000 residents, Bergen-Belsen was the largest camp of Jewish displaced persons in the British occupied zone. Under British military control, the camp was internally autonomous and became a close-knit Jewish society. Meanwhile, the Palestine issue, fuelled by strong Zionist sentiment among the DPs, created severe tension among the British authorities.

Thomas Rahe, director of the Bergen-Belsen Memorial, describes the social structure of life at the DP Camp Bergen-Belsen. The camp population was a melting pot of mainly young Jews with divergent customs and ideas. Most of the Holocaust survivors came from Poland and elsewhere in Eastern Europe. As a volunteer for the American Jewish Joint Distribution Committee, Zippy Orlin worked at Bergen-Belsen for two and a half years. At the end of July 1945, the Allies officially instructed the AJDC to organize relief efforts at the DP camps in occupied Germany. Sarah Kadosh, director of AJDC archives for Israel, describes the role and significance of the AJDC in arranging social assistance and care for the Jewish DPs. She has included Eric Nooter's observations in her article.

Genya Markon, formerly in charge of the photo archive of the United States Holocaust Memorial Museum (USHMM) and presently curator of the Collections Department at the museum, traced several individuals who appear on the photographs in the album of Zippy Orlin. The photographs help to structure the memories from this emotional period for those who were part of the camp. Genya Markon spoke with and recorded the reminiscences of Sally Bendremer Wideroff (AJDC social worker at Bergen-Belsen and Blankenese), John Fink (survivor and social worker in Bergen-Belsen), his wife Alice Fink (also a social worker; they were married at Bergen-Belsen), Reuma Schwartz Weizman (a social worker from Palestine), Hilde Jacobstahl Goldberg (a worker for the British Red Cross), Stefa Hasson (a Polish child survivor from Lodz) and Nandor Aron (a Rumanian survivor who was a policeman at the DP camp Bergen-Belsen). Brief texts throughout the book reflect their findings, as illustrated by photographs from the album.

Initially, little was known about Zippy's own experiences as an AJJDC volunteer at DP camp Bergen-Belsen. We obtained most of our information from interviews with her sister Bluma Rubin-Orlin and her brother Harry "Zvi" Orlin. Following the publication of the article mentioned above about Zippy and her photo album in the *NIOD Yearbook*, two articles by Miss C. Orlin surfaced from the *Zionist Record. The Organ of South African Jewry* from March 1949. After working in Bergen-Belsen, Zippy returned to South Africa, where she had lived since 1928. In "What it's really like in a D.P. Camp" and "Last step to Israel," Zippy described her memories of what is was like to live and work at DP Camp Bergen-Belsen. Her fascinating account is included here virtually without modifications. Remarkably, she does not mention her vast photo collection in the articles.

The *Exodus 47* was one of the sixty-five ships that transported Jewish DPs illegally to Palestine in the period between the Nazi capitulation and the proclamation of the State of Israel in May 1948. Many DPs from Bergen-Belsen were on board. The course of events concerning the *Exodus* became known all over the world. With the docks of Haifa in sight, the British authorities forced the ship to turn back. Upon arriving in Hamburg, the British made the desperate DPs disembark and three years after the war imprisoned them in heavily guarded

DP camps surrounded by barbed wire. The incident shocked the world. The photo album includes forty photographs by the professional photographer Ursula Litzmann, who lived in Hamburg at that time. She captured the emotional scenes of the disembarkation, the subsequent internment of the *Exodus* passengers and the infuriated reactions of the population of the DP camp Bergen-Belsen to the incidents.

From the outset, our intention was to publish the book in English. After all, the DP problem then was international. Most DPs emigrated to Israel and the United States after their internment in the camps in Germany, but some went to Canada and Australia. The relationship between the USHMM and the NIOD has been very close ever since the USHMM was established in 1993, also thanks to the long-term efforts and mediation by the Museum's Program Coordinator for Europe, Claus Müller.[7] In 1999 NIOD consulted the museum staff about the photo album. The USHMM was given permission to reproduce Zippy Orlin's entire album and to add the duplicates to its own collections. This publication has been made possible in part thanks to the material support and financial efforts by the USHMM. We are deeply grateful to the museum. We have also benifited greatly from the critical remarks that Severin Hochberg, researcher at the USHMM, made regarding the draft texts, and the close communication between Claus Müller and our staff in regard to this project.

The editors also thank all authors in this book for the contributions. Special thanks are due to Bluma Rubin-Orlin, Harry "Zvi" Orlin and Chaim Orlin († 1986). They helped preserve the album by their sister Zippy Orlin and have enabled us to feature her account and photographs in this book.

Liberation

Concentration camp Bergen-
Belsen shortly after the liberation
on April 15, 1945.

Concentration camp Bergen-
Belsen shortly after the liberation
on April 15, 1945.

To prevent the spread of typhus, the British authorities ordered that the wooden barracks of concentration camp Bergen-Belsen be burned down, May 21, 1945.

The Album and Zippy Orlin

Erik Somers and René Kok

Zippy Orlin's Bergen-Belsen photo album is an impressive historical legacy. The thirty-three pound volume is filled with 1,117 photographs that reflect a keen historical awareness and a very meticulous approach.

Cecillia "Zippy" Orlin was born in 1922 into a humble Jewish family in Siesiekeij in the Baltic state of Lithuania. At first there were four children in the family, and Zippy was the second.[1] The father, Yisrael Orlin, had difficulty supporting them. His brother, who had emigrated to South Africa in search of a better future, convinced him to follow with his family and build a new life at the other end of the world. In 1928 the Orlins journeyed to South Africa via Germany, where they soon became South African nationals. Yisrael Orlin earned a living by peddling fresh produce from a horse and cart in Johannesburg. His business did well: he was soon able to purchase a truck, and after a while had a thriving distribution business. In 1935 Chaim Orlin, the youngest child in the family, was born. Yiddish was the main language in the Orlin household, and all the children joined the Zionist youth movement *Habonim*.

In remote South Africa, the Orlins were safe from the horrors of World War II. Still, the war did not pass entirely unnoticed. Barney Orlin, the oldest of the five, served in the South African Army and fought in the battle for Tubruk. Zippy spent the war years as a secretary to the South African Jewish Board of Deputies, whose responsibilities included organizing social and cultural activities for the Jewish community in South Africa. Shortly after the war, in the spring of 1946, the Jewish War Appeal of the Jewish Board of Deputies invited Zippy to volunteer for the American Jewish Joint Distribution Committee (AJDC) to help the thousands of displaced Jewish survivors of Nazi atrocities at the former concentration camp Bergen-Belsen. Though inexperienced with relief work, Zippy's main asset in the view of the "Joint" was that her childhood in Lithuania made her fluent in Yiddish, besides her command of English. This was very useful indeed, since most of the residents at the DP Camp Bergen-Belsen were from Eastern Europe and spoke Yiddish regardless of their country of origin. After careful consideration, Zippy, then 24, agreed to go.

On May 21, 1946 the South African Jewish Board of Deputies and the Jewish War Appeal organized a splendid farewell banquet at the Carlton Hotel in Johannesburg in honor of the departures of Zippy and six fellow volunteers. At the occasion Mrs. M. Levitas said on behalf of those leaving: "it is a signal honor that we have been chosen for this noble work. We all will work in the knowledge that we are ambassadors of South Africa."[2]

Zippy Orlin at the DP Camp Bergen-Belsen

After a stop at the headquarters of the Joint Distribution Committee in Paris, Zippy reached Belsen in July 1946. She started working for the "Joint" during a period of major turmoil at the DP camp. The camp was initially a common residence for Jewish survivors and former non-Jewish forced labor recruits from Eastern Europe. Relations between the two groups were strained, and the former forced laborers were accused of having anti-Semitic sympathies.[3] The Central Committee of the Liberated Jews in the British Zone of Germany, which protected the interests of the Jewish DPs at Belsen, rejected the idea of ongoing coexistence. Despite resistance from the British Foreign Secretary Ernest Bevin, the committee prevailed in May 1946.

Henceforth, the DP camp Bergen-Belsen would accommodate Jewish DPs only. At that point a rigid internal Jewish organization emerged, and specific Jewish activities were arranged. The Central Committee, run by Josef Rosensaft, pursued a clear Zionist course. The aim was to emphasize individual Jewish identity, and daily life revolved around imminent departure for Israel, "the national homeland of the Jewish people." Contacts with the surrounding German population were virtually non-existent. Jewish DPs refused to seek employment at German firms on principle, and German civilians were prohibited from entering the camp.[4]

Zippy Orlin was part of a new crew of Joint staff recruited in haste and quickly trained to provide support at Bergen-Belsen.[5] After all, the DP camp had to absorb an unexpected crowd of Jews fleeing Eastern Europe because of the recent surge in anti-Semitic violence, especially in Poland, where a major pogrom took place in Kielce in July 1946. Within a few months, the camp population grew by more than two thousand. By July 1946, Bergen-Belsen had over ten thousand residents; in August the registered DP camp population peaked at 11,139.[6]

Zippy found the camp in massive disarray. The drastic increase in refugees had left the relief resources sorely inadequate in all respects. The facilities available were far from sufficient. Without taking the time to absorb the overwhelming impressions, Zippy immediately went to work. Her chief responsibility was to care for the very youngest children at the camp. In early 1946 there were 880 children between 6 and 18. Because of the influx of Jewish refugees from Poland and Hungary, their number increased very rapidly. In addition, many babies were born at the camp. In 1948 the thousandth birth was registered there. The total number of children at Belsen ultimately reached 2,300, including approximately 1,000 under three.[7]

As the hope for the future, children were idolized at Belsen. Raising them received careful consideration. The first school opened in mid June 1945. Most teachers were DPs themselves. Instruction stressed Zionism: Hebrew and lessons about Palestine were important parts of the curriculum.[8] In October 1946 a kindergarten and elementary school opened in Barracks RB 7 for the very youngest children. The school was run by the AJDC, and Zippy was appointed one of the staff. In addition, she and several co-workers cared for dozens of young orphans. Zippy was highly dedicated and devoted a large section of the album to child care.

The children's activity program ran from nine thirty in the morning until four o'clock in the afternoon. In addition to learning about hygiene and table manners, they were taught self-sufficiency and responsibility. The older ones designated a group leader, who kept order and discipline in the classroom. Once a month an AJDC physician examined the students.

Although Zippy Orlin was initially assigned to care for the orphans, she appears in some photographs in the album to have served with the camp hospital nursing staff as well. Several photographs depict young TB patients at AJDC sanitariums in Merano, Italy, and in Davos, Switzerland, hoping to recuperate their strength in the spring of 1947. Zippy accompanied the children on the journey and spent a few days with them. One of the few documents from that period about Zippy is a letter from the children in Merano thanking her for her care and attention: "Taking us to Merano you provided the basis for our healthy future. We assure you that every one of us understands your action. There is no proportion between words of thanks and your action. You should be proud of your work. We shall keep you in our thoughts forever."[9]

Zippy helped the few children given leave by the British authorities to go to Palestine prepare for their departure. In March 1947 residents throughout the camp rejoiced at the news that the British had issued 500 exit certificates to Jewish orphans. In the days preceding their departure, Zippy Orlin and her co-workers were busy making travel arrangements and organizing a farewell celebration for the children, who would leave for Palestine by train via Marseille on March 12, 1947. She took a series of photographs of her pupils the day of the emotional farewell. In her album she described them as the "lucky few." That same month the British announced that Jewish DPs would henceforth

Zippy Orlin and her co-worker and friend, "Willy with the Leica," who worked at the Transport Unit (HQ 7). Summer, 1947. Willy took an unknown number of the photographs in the album.

receive between four and five hundred exit permits every month. The permits were intended exclusively for residents of DP camp Belsen, although the Central Committee felt an obligation to share them with other Jewish DPs in Germany as well.[10]

In her report about her activities at the camp, Zippy wrote about the exercise group that she organized twice a week for the women. She convinced the women, who were somewhat reluctant at first, of the importance of physical exercise and got them interested. Togetherness and compassion were the foundations of camp social life. Both the camp population and the AJDC had only each other for company during their leisure hours. Since contact with the German population was to be avoided as much as possible, entertainments were organized internally. Zippy was involved in the many social activities at the camp. The album includes photographs of celebrations and other festive occasions that she attended. Zippy enjoyed the motley company of volunteers from all corners of the world. Whenever a staff member departed, a farewell party was organized. Occasional excursions were arranged as well. Photographs depict a delightful evening at the British officers' club in Hamburg, a summer day on the banks of the Aller River, and New Year's Eve 1947 with friends in snow-covered Bad Harzberg.

People interested in escaping the daily camp routine participated in sporting events and attended theater performances. Zippy was present at all weddings and celebrations of new births, which were regular events. Weddings of Joint staff members and other workers were particularly festive occasions with much singing and dancing.[11]

Zippy Orlin amid DP children
at "Oneg Shabbath".

Departure

Zippy finished working for the Joint in late 1948. Her departure from Belsen coincided with the change in status of the DP camp and the rapid decline in the number of residents. The population had decreased by half since Zippy started working there in the summer of 1946.[12] Following the proclamation of the State of Israel, immigration to the "Promised Land" soared in 1948. The DP camp became a transit camp: Belsen was a center for organizing and registering departures to Israel. The activities still in progress increasingly revolved around the preparations for departure. As the AJDC gradually became less indispensable to the DPs, all AJDC operations in the British Zone were suspended the next year. The Joint transferred its responsibilities to the Hebrew Immigrant Aid Society.[13]

In early September 1948 Zippy learned that she was free to leave after having spent over two years at Belsen. She received a final performance evaluation, and the American AJDC director at Belsen, Samuel Dallob, drafted a report about her.[14] Her overall performance was rated as "very good." The administration was particularly impressed with her "application of energy, interest, skills, initiative, resourcefulness" and especially with her "cooperativeness and her ability to work with others." She scored slightly lower in "knowledge of particular field of work and of the fundamentals on which it is based" and on "analytical ability; constructive reasoning in the field of her specialization." This was hardly surprising, since Zippy was virtually untrained in social work. The only minor point of criticism in the report was the remark: "over-identification with clients," although this comment reveals that she was very dedicated.

Zippy worked at Belsen for 27 months. Uninhibited and practically inexperienced, she had accepted the challenge of traveling to Bergen-Belsen to do social work in the summer of 1946. She found the period emotionally taxing but also very enlightening and described it as "crammed with hard work, interesting encounters with the remnants of European Jewry, and a host of invigorating experiences. I shared their joys and sorrows, listened to the gruesome tales they told, discussed their problems with them, and during the course of time became part of the life they led in Belsen."[15]

In December 1948 Zippy Orlin boarded a ship bound for Israel. After a brief stay in the new state, she traveled on to South Africa in January or February 1949. Upon her return, she started writing about her experiences. On March 4, 1949, the South African periodical, *The Zionist Record*, published the first of two episodes about Zippy's experiences entitled "A South African Girl in Belsen. What it's really like in a D.P. Camp." She must have started assembling the photo album shortly after her return as well.

The Photo Album

The photo album is a diverse collection of amateur photographs that Zippy compiled with great care. With little concern for chronological order, she arranged the photographs by theme and added brief captions in English. Unfortunately, these captions are rather general. The names of the individuals depicted are indicated in only a few cases. The research on the collection included careful removal of each photograph from the album to examine if there were any notes on the reverse side. In several cases this search yielded interesting information that was complemented with data from archival research, interviews, and the literature. Nonetheless, the identities of the individuals on the photographs often remain unknown, as well as when and sometimes where the photographs were taken.

The 1,117 photographs are impressive. Although the photo archive of the Netherlands Institute for War Documentation (NIOD) was vast before the album was donated, the collection did not include a single photograph of the DP camp Bergen-Belsen. Thanks to this acquisition, the NIOD now has the largest collection on the post-war history of the camp. Other institutions with photographs of the DP camp include Yad Vashem in Jerusalem, the documentation center of the Gedankstätte Bergen-Belsen, the archives department and records of the AJDC in New York, the United States Holocaust Memorial Museum in Washington, D.C., and the Imperial War Museum in London.

Zippy Orlin probably did not take all the photographs in the album herself. Most appear to have been given to her by co-workers and DPs. The album features a diverse selection of portrait photographs that she was given to remember people by or in exchange for a picture of herself. One of the photographers, described as Willy with the Leica, was a co-worker she befriended who worked

Zippy Orlin and her co-worker
Harry Kopp.

at the transport unit (HQ 7). She wrote a caption: "Willy comes over with his camera and takes some crazy snapshots."[16] Harry Kopp, who worked with the same transport unit, took photographs that are found in the album as well.

Zippy filled the first two pages in the album with pictures commemorating the period that Bergen-Belsen was a concentration camp. She intended the photographs as a tribute to the victims who were murdered: "They are no more. The road to death for 30,000," reads her caption here. Her caption to a photograph of the sign, "Here lies buried 2500 bodies," reads: "The end of the journey." The photographs reveal that a monument and tombstones now stand where barracks once were, and that bushes and trees have begun to grow: "Amongst the rubble a tree now grows. That we shall reme[m]ber: Jews, Christians. The known and the unknown" (page 1 of the album). In the weeks following the liberation in 1945, the British burned the concentration camp buildings to the ground because of the typhus epidemic. The DP camp was adjacent to the concentration camp site in a well-equipped military complex, which had housed the *Wehrmacht Truppenübungsplatz* and later served to house the camp SS personnel as well. Photographs in the album depicting the complex shortly after the war precede the scenes of life at the DP camp. Zippy wrote: "1945. The SS torture[r]s move out and the tortured remnants move in" (p. 2). The rest of the album radiates the new, resilient society that emerged on the site once filled with death and persecution. The following photo collage shows the many aspects of camp life and the recovering camp inmates in a nutshell:"They wanted: to live, to provide, to be a child, to play, to keep law and order, to feast, to celebrate and to care for soul and body" (p. 3).

The album also describes the physical recovery of the children at the camp infirmary (p. 4). Photographs depict the library ("In the library was food for the hungry minds") and the editors and publishers of the camp weekly *Unzere Stimme* (p. 5). The album contains an extensive photographic record of the vocational school and the many occupations the young people were taught (p. 6). Another page in the album depicts an *Oneg Sabbath* celebration (p. 7) and another an *Oneg Sabbath* celebration for Jewish orphans on which Zippy herself appears. Her caption reflects the desire to impart a sense of Jewish identity: "To those who had lived in monasteries and nunneries, *Oneg Sabbath* was a new and delightful experience. They returned to Judaism with pride and joy" (p. 23). The caption to the photographs of a Chanukah celebration reads: "They revelled in the spirit of Chanukah. With heads held high, they faced the future with determination. They were among friends at last!" (p. 26).

Several pages in the album feature scenes of the kindergarten (R.B. 7), where the very youngest children from the camp were brought (by bus in some cases). The captions indicate that Zippy and her co-workers aimed to make the children feel safe, to help them learn to enjoy life again and to cultivate their sense of self-esteem. The pages in the photo album contain texts such as: "Sturdy little toddlers romped and played in the flower-covered fields and expressed the childish emotions so long suppressed" and "by love, tears make way for joy, crying makes way for singing, repression gives way to expression" (p. 12). The caption to photographs of a children's performance reads: "coming one step nearer to regaining their individuality yet retaining the group spirit" (p. 13). In a photo report about a large group of orphans Zippy wrote: "From every corner of wartorn Europe were brought the orphans. Some born in deathcamps, others adopted by self-sacrificing Christians and yet others brought up by fear-less partisans" (p. 19) and "These children whose envir[o]nment had for several years been a nightmare of fears and frustrations, hate and distrust found the love and freedom of R.B. 7 a strange, new experience (p. 20). On one of the next pages Zippy wrote: "The staff of R.B. 7 worked untiringly and experienced much patience: restoring to the children faith in humanity and the courage to look and plan ahead" (p. 22).

Throughout the album are photographs of sports competitions, theatrical performances and festive evenings. The caption to the photographs of a youth performance at the camp theater reads: "Acting and singing gave expression to their regained lust for life" (p. 5).

The album also includes a detailed visual report of the stay of several older children from Belsen at the Warburg Children's Health-Home of the Joint at Blankenese. "Busloads of Belsen-children arrived for a well-earned holiday" (pp. 29-33). The aforementioned stay of 56 TB patients from Bergen-Belsen at the Joint sanitarium at Merano in Italy was photographed extensively as well. The group traveled to Hanover in Red Cross vehicles and continued the journey by train. One of the pages features a great many portraits, where Zippy wrote: "some faces I will never forget" (pp. 57-63). Sixteen photographs depict another group of TB patients staying at the spa, Mon Repos, at Davos in Switzerland (p. 64). Zippy was probably not there in person.

There is also an impressive report of the transport of 500 orphans to Palestine authorized by the British. These included many children from Bergen-Belsen (pp. 35-42). The photographs depict the preparations, as well as the farewell celebration ("The farewell party at which joy and sadness mingled"), packing ("Suitcases are packed. The orphans left Belsen well equipped; from a pair of solid boots to a scooter") and the departing children dressed in new clothes and waving from the Belsen platform ("Shalom, shalom lehitraot").

There are also pictures of special events that took place in the camp, such as the elections of the Jewish Central Committee – "Belsen goes to the polls – Zionist elections 1947" (p. 45), the Labor Day celebration on May 1, activities of the Second Congress of Liberated Jews in the British Zone, which took place partly in Warburg and in the camp in July 1947, and the annual commemoration of tens of thousands of victims of the concentration camp at the anniversary of its liberation on 15 April.

The first authorized transport of DPs from the camp to the new State of Israel in 1948 was a memorable event. Three hundred adults and children were allowed to participate: "The chosen 300 get a grand send-off from their less [un]fortunate [sic] friends, who must wait their turn," wrote Zippy alongside the photographs (pp. 53-56).

Many photographs in the album depict the people that Zippy worked with and spent her leisure time with every day. The pictures reveal the close bond that formed under the difficult circumstances in which people depended on each other (pp. 65-92). One of the highlights was the wedding reception of Joint worker Hans Finke with Jewish Relief Unit staff member Alice Redlich: "Alice JRU marries Hans AJDC and the whole camp joins in the celebrations" (p. 88).

The album ends with press photographs by Ursula Litzmann, who captured the dramatic debarkation of the passengers from the Exodus 47 in Hamburg. The compelling scenes depict the accommodation of the distraught and exhausted passengers in DP camps surrounded by barbed wire and guarded by British soldiers and the severe indignation that the affair instigated at DP camp Bergen-Belsen (pp. 93-110).

Conclusion

Zippy Orlin cherished the heavy photo album for years. Following her return from Bergen-Belsen, she resided briefly in South Africa before traveling to London. There she trained as a beautician and specialized in facial massage. Although Zippy returned to South Africa again, she was seized by the urge to help build the Jewish state. In 1960 she settled in Israel, where she became a practicing beautician.

Her younger brother "Zvi" had settled in Israel earlier. He remembers his sister as "a very outgoing personality; full of pep. She was a good cook and loved to entertain friends, many of who were married. She was very well dressed, had a good figure and looked like a model. She had many people who were devoted to her."[17] Zippy never married.

In early 1980 Zippy Orlin fell ill with an incurable disease. She spent the last months of her life with her sister Bluma Rubin-Orlin in Johannesburg, South Africa. She died there at age 58 on September 1, 1980.

Among her personal possessions in Israel her brother Chaim found the collection of photographs from Bergen-Belsen. He took the album home to Amsterdam, his home since 1950, with him. On Friday September 19, 1986, he entrusted the photo album to the Netherlands Institute for War Documentation.

Camp life

Young mothers in the summer of 1947.

Doing paperwork at the infirmary.   *"Hagibor – boys' Pesach 1947"*

Kitchen at the Belsen Children's
home in R.B. 7.

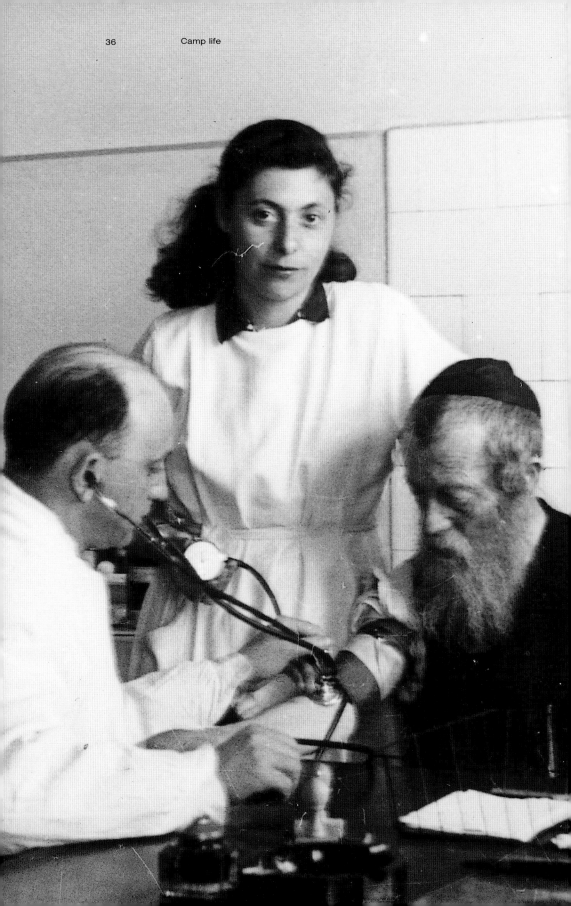

"The Sick Bay was always a hive of activity. Here minor ailments were attended to and pills and mixtures dispensed." Dr. Weinberg of the AJDC.

"With heads held high, they faced the future."

Bread rations.

Composing room of the camp daily *Undzer Sztyme*.

Rafael Olevski (left), editor of *Undzer Sztyme* and head of the Cultural Department.

Rabbi Joel Halpern (center) signs a document. Rabbi Israel Moshe Olewski (right) and an unknown man look on.

AJDC headquarters of volunteer associations, welfare department. Left: Vida Kaufman.

Jewish DP policemen consisting of camp inmates. Far right, in plain clothes: Police Chief Winek.

DP Camp 1945-1950: The British Section

Angelika Königseder and Juliane Wetzel

To this day the memory of Bergen-Belsen concentration camp, located north of Hannover and run by the Nazis from late April 1943 to 15 April 1945, permeates the story of the largest camp for Jewish displaced persons, which existed there until 1951.[1] Until March 1944 the Bergen-Belsen detention camp had been an internment center for Jews who either had influential connections in enemy countries or had been designated as "exchange Jews" to be traded for German citizens. As a result, conditions there were more tolerable than at other concentration camps. This changed radically in the course of 1944, when increasing numbers of prisoners who were unfit for work, physically depleted, and seriously ill were transferred to Bergen-Belsen from other camps. When Josef Kramer, the former commander of Auschwitz-Birkenau, assumed control of the camp in December 1944, Bergen-Belsen officially became a concentration camp. As a transit and reception camp, it was exceptional among the Nazi concentration camps. After Kramer's arrival, the many incoming "evacuation transports" swelled the camp population from around 15,000 to about 60,000 at the time of the liberation, despite the estimated 35,000 deaths.[2] As a result, the care facilities collapsed, and a devastating typhus epidemic broke out.

Upon liberating the camp on April 15, 1945, the British soldiers encountered horrific scenes. Brigadier-General H.L. Glyn Hughes, Deputy Director of Medical Services, Second British Army, who organized immediate medical care for the survivors, described the dreadful conditions confronting the soldiers as follows:

No description nor photograph could really bring home the horror that was outside the huts, and the frightful scenes inside were much worse. There were various sizes of piles of corpses lying all over the camp... The compounds

themselves had bodies lying about in them. The gutters were full and within
the huts there were uncountable number of bodies, some even in the same
bunks as the living.[3]

Unlike the liberators of nearly all other concentration and extermination camps,
the troops entering Bergen-Belsen witnessed a mass of dead bodies. There
were an estimated 10,000 unburied corpses. In the weeks that followed over
13,000 former prisoners died despite all the medical efforts. Death remained
an everyday occurrence for quite a while. One survivor explained the difference.
Although far more people had died at Auschwitz-Birkenau, death was visible and
tangible at Bergen-Belsen: "In Birkenau entire groups would simply disappear...
In Bergen-Belsen... you died slowly, from illness, exhaustion, cold, most from
hunger... In Bergen-Belsen you stared death in the face at every moment."[4]

The first concern of the British liberators was to provide care and stem
the typhus epidemic. Between April 24 and May 21, 1945 Camp I (the former
concentration camp) was evacuated, the infested barracks were torn down,
and the remainder was burned on May 21. Prior to the liberation, Camp II had
absorbed the overflow from Camp I. Together with Camp III, it contained the
southern and northern barracks of the nearby exercise site for the troops,
while Camp IV consisted of the former officers' quarters. The Bergen-Belsen
DP Camp Hohne was established in these three sections. Although the British
named it DP Camp Hohne, the Jewish survivors continued to call it DP Camp
Belsen in memory of the horrors of Bergen-Belsen concentration camp.

Only after the countless bodies were buried and the area separated from
the site of the former concentration camp did the horrific confrontation with
the mass murder become less acute. Simultaneously, the typhus epidemic
stopped. Despite the limited resources and the upheaval, the British soon
managed to provide immediate care for the survivors. Many sources describe
the pride of the liberators in this considerable achievement.[5]

Within a few days of the liberation, the survivors formed into national groups
to protect their interests. The DPs from Western Europe wanted to return
quickly to their home countries, in keeping with the objectives of the occupying
forces. Repatriating the former prisoners from Eastern Europe was more
complicated. Because of their political opposition to the new Communist
regimes or their fear of reprisals for actual or perceived collaboration with the
National Socialists, they did not want to be repatriated. Moreover, repatriation
to their former homes in Eastern Europe was not a realistic possibility for most
of the Jewish survivors. The thriving Jewish communities had been destroyed;
the antisemitism that continued unabated after the war doomed any attempt at
restoration.

This led to the central conflict that permeated relations between the British
and the Jewish survivors in the years that followed. In keeping with their histori-

cally progressive ideology, the British considered National Socialism to be less a Jewish than a humanitarian catastrophe. Because of their mistaken assessment of National Socialist racial policy and its consequences, the British did not recognize the Jews as persecution victims. Under no circumstances were Jews granted preferential treatment. Unlike the Americans in their zone, the British regarded the Jews not as a genuine group of Displaced Persons but merely as subjects of their countries of origin. A memorandum from the British chief of staff explains this position: *It is undesirable to accept the Nazi theory that the Jews are a separate race. Jews, in common with all other religious sects, should be treated according to their nationality rather than as a race or a religious sect... Jews should be accommodated in camps appropriate to their nationality rather than to their race or religion. Any form of racial or religious segregation will only give rise to anti-Jewish feeling and may well have far-reaching repercussions.*[6]

The strained rapprochement between the Jewish DPs and the military and the delayed arrival of the Jewish relief organizations soon convinced the survivors that they needed to organize and build their future themselves.[7] Three days after the liberation at Belsen, Josef Rosensaft formed an initial provisional committee of liberated Jews with nine other survivors, including his future wife Hadassa Bimko and Rabbi Zvi Asaria (Helfgott). The committee made its first official appearance at the first congress of the *She'erit Hapletah* (the remainder of the rescued, as the Jewish survivors called themselves) in the British Zone held on September 25-27, 1945, and then continued its work with the same members. Rosensaft, who was born in Bendzin, Poland in 1911 and had owned a foundry there, had survived the Auschwitz and Mittelbau-Dora concentration camps and had arrived at Bergen-Belsen concentration camp on an evacuation transport in early April 1945. The most important objectives of the new committee were to help those who had been liberated recover their health, ensure hygienic conditions, locate surviving relatives, and achieve political rights. The Jewish committee soon became an important operator at the camp since it represented the largest number of residents at Belsen. The committee also tried to represent all Jewish survivors in the British Zone. In keeping with their policy, the British refused to recognize the committee as an official negotiating partner.

The Harrison Report

During the period immediately after liberation the American occupying forces also did not consider the special needs of Jewish survivors in their zone. Barbed wire and guards at the DP camps were standard military procedure. They guaranteed order, control, and protection. The military did not consider the memories these methods would revive among the survivors or the feelings they would evoke. In the American Zone the Harrison Report issued in the

View of DP camp Bergen-Belsen.   *"The SS torturers move out, and the tortured remnants move in."*

summer of 1945 raised awareness and horrified responses in the United States and ultimately brought about a change in policy. Shocked at the critical reports in the American media, U.S. President Harry S. Truman launched an investigation into the prevailing rumors about mistreatment of survivors at the camps.
Earl G. Harrison, the former U.S. Commissioner for Immigration, was sent by the U.S. government to Europe in July 1945. He visited some 30 DP camps in Germany and Austria and on August 24, 1945 he presented his report. A milestone in American DP policy, it also had sweeping consequences for Jews living in the British Zone and for British policy on Palestine. Harrison's critique was as follows: *Many Jewish displaced persons... living under guard behind barbed-wire fences (built by the Germans for slave-laborers and Jews) including some of the most notorious concentration camps, amidst crowded, frequently unsanitary and generally grim conditions, in complete idleness, with no opportunity, except surreptitiously, to communicate with the outside world, waiting, hoping for some word of encouragement and action in their behalf... Many of the Jewish displaced persons, late in July, had no clothing other than their concentration camp garb – a rather hideous striped pajama effect – while others, to their chagrin, were obliged to wear German S.S. uniforms. It is questionable which clothing they hate more.* [8]

One important outcome of the report was the awareness that additional aid was feasible only if the Jewish survivors were recognized as Jews. Harrison was very explicit on this point: *The first and plainest need of these people is a recognition of their actual status and by this I mean their status as Jews... While SHAEF (now Combined Displaced Person Executive) policy directives have recognized formerly persecuted persons, including enemy and ex-enemy nationals, as one of the special categories of displaced persons, the general practice thus far has been to follow only nationality lines. While admittedly it is not normally desirable to set aside particular racial or religious groups from their nationality categories, the plain truth is that this was done for so long by the Nazis that a group has been created which has special needs. Jews as Jews (not as members of their nationality groups) have been more severely victimized than the non-Jewish members of the same or other nationalities... Refusal to recognize the Jews as such has the effect, in this situation, of closing one's eyes to their former and more barbaric persecution... I recommend urgently that separate camps be set up for Jews.[9]*

General Dwight D. Eisenhower, the commander in chief of the American forces of occupation in Germany, was informed by President Truman and responded immediately to Harrison's objections, ordering that the camps be equipped to serve as exclusive accommodations for Jewish DPs. Pressured by the Americans and by Belsen's Jewish committee, the British government issued a confidential directive authorizing separate housing units for Jews but prohibiting a Jewish camp as such.[10] At Belsen, which held 60 percent of the Jewish DPs in the British Zone at the time, the military government arranged exclusively Jewish housing units in Camp IV and Camp V, which had recently opened as well. Jews continued to live with non-Jews in Camps II and III. Arranging a separate housing unit had been one of the Belsen committee's top priorities. The change in British policy resulted from outside pressure. It was the the new situation in the U.S. Zone rather than their own decision which resulted in concessions to the survivors.

Another consequence of the Harrison report was the appointment of an advisor on Jewish Affairs for the U.S. Army to mediate between the military and the Jewish DPs. The strength of character of the seven consecutive advisors from August 1945 until the end of 1949 made them very effective advocates for the Jewish survivors with the military authorities. After some delay, an Advisor on Jewish Affairs was appointed for the British Zone in March 1946. Unlike in the American Zone, however, this advisor reported not to the military but to the British government, and was therefore based at the control office in London. The minimal prestige associated with this new position was apparent from its lack of support staff. This situation, combined with the complicated political circumstances surrounding the Palestine Mandate, made conditions decidedly unfavorable for the advisor to accomplish his mission. The person holding this office (the lawyer Colonel Robert Bernard Solomon) had been president of the Jewish National Fund in Great Britain until 1937, and was known as an ardent Zionist. The British military government was suspicious of him from the outset.

Cecil E. Steel, a member of the Control Commission for Germany British Element, expressed his reservations to the Foreign Office in a confidential letter of October 1946:

It is probably a pity a Jew was ever appointed 'Jewish Adviser'. Almost any honest Jew will admit that no Jew can be really objective about Jewish affairs; and anyone who is not objective cannot be expected to advise H.M.G. reliably... I am not suggesting we should necessarily try to get Solomon replaced at present, though if he commits any serious gaff we may have to do so.[11]

This assessment arose from the fundamental differences between British policy and the objectives of Solomon, who shared the Zionist views of the Jewish DPs. After failing in all his efforts to obtain additional certificates for entry to Palestine and having become demoralized in his commitment to the DPs as a result of the constant setbacks, he resigned in April 1947. Although Solomon remained in office at the request of leading Zionists – probably until his death in the spring of 1948[12] – he was far less influential than the advisors in the American Zone.

The call in the Harrison Report for 100,000 additional immigration certificates to Palestine was also a political bombshell for the bilateral relations between the United States and Great Britain. According to Harrison, Palestine offered the only true solution to the Jewish DP problem: *Most Jews want to leave Germany and Austria as soon as possible. That is their first and great expressed wish and while this report necessarily deals with other needs present in the situation, many of the people themselves fear other suggestions of plans for their benefit because of the possibility that attention might thereby be diverted from the all-important matter of evacuation from Germany... They want to be evacuated to Palestine now, just as other national groups are being repatriated to their homes... The Jewish Agency for Palestine has submitted to the British Government a petition that one hundred thousand additional certificates be made available... No other single matter is, therefore, so important from the viewpoint of Jews in Germany and Austria and those elsewhere who have known the horrors of the concentration camps as is the disposition of the Palestine question.*[13]

The most important long-term consequence of the Harrison Report was its acknowledgment of Palestine's central significance for the Jewish DPs. Samuel Gringauz, a lawyer from Kovno and chairman of the board of the Landsberg DP Camp in the American Zone, explained:

Empowered by its own martyrdom and the legacy left it by the dead, the Sherit Hapleita... demands of the Jewish people a single and united national-political attitude. This is the basic foundation of the Zionism of the survivors. It is no party Zionism; it is a historical-philosophical Zionism felt as an historical mission, as a debt to the dead, as retribution toward the enemy, as a duty to the living.

It is, moreover, a Zionism of warning, because the Sherit Hapleita feels that the continuation of Jewish national abnormality means the danger of a repetition of the catastrophe.[14]

Relaxing the rigid British immigration restrictions – a mere 1,500 certificates were issued worldwide every month – seemed the sole satisfactory solution. Great Britain, however, had no intention of abandoning all remaining strongholds of its remaining global empire. After being forced to grant independence to India in January 1948, Great Britain wanted to avoid weakening its position in the Near East and causing Arab sabotage campaigns, which the British believed would be the necessary consequence of raising the immigration quota.

The Bevin Statement and the Anglo-American Committee of Inquiry

The recommendation by U.S. President Truman in late August 1945 to Great Britain that 100,000 Jews be admitted to Palestine gave rise to a long-standing British-American disagreement that made the two nations treat the Jewish DPs differently in their respective zones. The British clearly distinguished between DP policy and Palestine policy. In September the British followed Foreign Secretary Bevin's suggestion that the limit of 1,500 immigration certificates a month be maintained. The justification was fear of attacks from the Arabs, who were considered to be far more powerful than the Jews of Palestine. The British expected little resistance from the supposedly weaker, Jewish side. Immediately following the disclosure of the British position, however, Jewish terror actions started, directed against British targets and heralding the long, fierce struggle to open the gates of Palestine to the Jews that culminated in the establishment of the State of Israel on May 14, 1948.[15]

American disapproval of the restrictive British policy, documented in the correspondence between Great Britain and the United States,[16] did not lead the British to change their DP policy. Jews were granted no privileges whatsoever. Unlike in the American Zone, they were not considered a separate group of DPs but were categorized according to their respective nationalities. Emigration destinations were to be found as quickly as possible for Jews that could not be repatriated. The United States was considered particularly responsible in this respect. The British pursued this strategy to disassociate the fate of the liberated Jews in Europe from the political rise of Palestine. When the British Foreign Secretary Ernest Bevin stated at a press conference that after all the Jews were not the only victims of fascism, anti-British demonstrations were staged by DPs throughout Germany and Austria.[17] The committee of liberated Jews in Belsen organized a protest campaign and submitted a resolution to the British government in which they requested "not to prolong our bitter existence in camps. Give us the possibility to live free lives in our home in Eretz Israel (Palestine)."[18] The British military government immediately imposed sanctions on the protesters by eliminating the food rations of those who did not report to work on the day of the incident. This increased the acrimony of the Jewish-British disagreement.

Bevin had issued his statement (which made him a *persona non grata* with the Zionist movement) at a press conference after the session of Parliament on November 13, 1945, the very day that the Anglo-American Committee of Inquiry regarding the problems of European Jewry and Palestine was established in a concerted effort between American and British negotiators. In the early months of 1946, the commission visited various DP camps, including Belsen, as well as the Near East, to learn about the emigration plans of the surviving Jews and to fulfill them. Even though the commission comprised equal numbers of British and Americans, Foreign Secretary Bevin expected the outcome to favor Great Britain. To Great Britain's dismay, however, the commission report presented in April 1946 approved Truman's recommendation that 100,000 Jews be admitted to Palestine immediately.[19]

The report gave the Jewish survivors new hope, although it hardly improved relations between the inhabitants of Belsen and the British authorities. The vehement criticism of Josef Rosensaft with respect to the British DP policy had been a frequent source of irritation for quite a while. The British considered Rosensaft to be "a continual source of trouble."[20] They were particularly annoyed at the ingratitude of the representatives of the Jewish survivors for the devoted care that the British were so proud to have provided during the initial weeks following the liberation of Bergen-Belsen concentration camp. The Jewish DPs, however, had entirely different expectations. Under no circumstances were they willing to acknowledge the legitimacy of any British demands. In particular, the Jews blamed the British for failing to help them during the war. The speech by Norbert Wollheim, the deputy chairman of the Jewish interest board, at the inauguration of a central memorial stone at Belsen in April 1946 epitomized this view. He accused the British (his use of English was no coincidence) of refraining from any action against the mass murder of the Jews, despite their knowledge of the German actions; they should be ashamed of themselves. Wollheim also deplored the ongoing suffering of the Jews since their liberation. This would end only when the British government opened the gates of Palestine.[21] The British authorities at the Belsen DP Camp regarded Wollheim's statements as sheer provocation, and were determined to initiate sanctions against the deputy chairman of the committee. It was probably thanks to the British Advisor on Jewish Affairs Colonel Solomon that such a response was never actually forthcoming.[22]

Relations between the Jewish Committee and the British and between the United States and Great Britain were sorely tested again with the start of the mass exodus from Eastern Europe to the Western occupation zones in Germany and Austria in 1946. This flight was instigated by the antisemitic incidents primarily in Poland, which culminated in 42 Jews murdered in the Kielce pogrom on July 4, 1946. Illegal Jewish escape organizations guided a major portion of these refugees to the American occupation zones in Germany and Austria, not only because the Americans responded – despite the resistance of some military personnel[23] – by opening the borders of their zones, but also because those helping the refugees hoped this mass immigration would lead the Americans to pressure the British to open the gates of Palestine. From February 18, 1946 onward, all Jews reaching the American occupation zone were treated as DPs and were entitled to accommodations, food, and clothing, even though the refugees from Eastern Europe did not fit the original definition of DPs. (The definition was restricted to individuals who had been driven from their home during the war.) Great Britain had no intention whatsoever of emulating the liberal American disposition. The American willingness to accept refugees in their zone made British Palestine policy seem absurd. The British dismissed the reports about the difficulties facing Jews in Poland, antisemitic outrages, and discrimination as false horror stories spread by the Jewish refugee relief organizations to influence the survivors.

While no more than 15,000 Jews ever stayed in the camps in the British Zone, the American military authorities had to accommodate a mass influx of over 140,000 Jewish DPs in their camps. In the French Zone, however, only about 1,000 Jews were in the DP camps and at smaller agricultural training sites. In the zone under Soviet occupation, the DP problem was never officially acknowledged, and Jewish survivors were not attributed any special status.

While far more than 100,000 Jews from Eastern Europe were absorbed in the American Zone, only a few thousand "infiltrees" in the British Zone were initially sent to Belsen. They were not recognized as DPs there, since they were unable to present the required proof that they had been in Germany at the time of the liberation. Most new immigrants were thus the responsibility of the German authorities and were not entitled to DP camp accommodations or extra rations. Many Jewish immigrants from Eastern Europe nevertheless obtained "illegal" refuge at Belsen, where they relied on the Jewish Committee and the "legal" DPs. The British vehemently condemned this independent course of action on the part of the Jewish representatives: the conflict was in danger of escalating. The acting military government commanding officer in Belsen Captain McAllen feared that the military government might lose control of the camp. He firmly – and rightly – believed that Belsen was being used as an illegal transit station for the refugees from Eastern Europe en route to Palestine. Even the relief organizations, such as the American Jewish Joint Distribution Committee (AJDC), the British Jewish Relief Unit (JRU), as well as the United Nations refugee organization, the United Nations Relief and Rehabilitation Administration (UNRRA), acted against the British policy by providing the refugees with logistical support.

While McAllen's assessment was essentially accurate, his effort to reprimand

Josef Rosensaft as an individual caused problems. Accusing Rosensaft of being a communist and working closely with the Soviet military government not only perpetuated the long-standing stereotype that equated Jews with communists but also suggested a frenzied search for grounds to discredit them as negotiating partners or official representatives of the Jewish survivors. Representatives of the Political Division of the military government went further still and talked earnestly about how they could rid themselves of Rosensaft, the "chief nigger in the woodpile."[24] The issues mattered less than the direct attacks against Josef Rosensaft, and Norbert Wollheim. Rosensaft's criticism of British policy, which was ignited by actual abuses and the lack of prospects for the survivors, received no consideration but was simply dismissed as griping. This position was reflected in a letter to the Foreign Office of September 1946: "The difficulties our authorities have had in dealing with the Jewish DPs in the British Zone are in large measure attributable to him."[25] The ongoing political humiliation steadily reduced Rosensaft's willingness to compromise with the British.

In the summer of 1946, relations between the Belsen DPs and the British authorities reached their nadir. Incidents occurring outside the sphere of influence of the two parties to the conflict made for increasing acrimony. While the Jewish wave of refugees from Eastern Europe worsened the situation in Germany's western zones of occupation, the terror attacks of the Jewish underground organization Irgun Zvi Leumi in Palestine assumed a new order of magnitude with the attack on the King David Hotel (the British military headquarters) that killed 91 people in Jerusalem on July 22. The British immediately tightened restrictions both in Palestine and in their zones of occupation. The British high commissioner in Palestine urged the government in London to halt the illegal immigration, since the underground organization kept recruiting more members from the new arrivals. After heated discussions with the general staff, the government decided on August 7, 1946 that illegal immigrants to Palestine would be interned on Cyprus. Within a week the first 1,200 refugees from Haifa were transferred to Cyprus.

The Exodus Affair

Worn down by the political course of events, the British government in London decided on February 14, 1947 to return the Palestine Mandate to the United Nations; the United Nations subsequently formed a Special Committee on Palestine (UNSCOP) to find a solution to the Palestine conflict and the future of the Jewish DPs. Following discussions in Europe and the United States, the members of UNSCOP traveled to Palestine for a first-hand impression of the situation in the summer of 1947. The hair-raising Exodus Affair occurred around this time. The *Exodus 47* was one of 65 illegal vessels that transported Jews from Europe to Palestine between the end of World War II and the establishment of the State of Israel in May 1948. Most refugees started their journeys on vessels

DPs commemorate the victims of the Nazi camp Bergen-Belsen on the former campgrounds, April 15, 1947.

that were rarely seaworthy and ended them in internment camps in Palestine and on Cyprus. On July 10, 1947 the *Exodus 47* weighed anchor from the French harbor of Sète near Marseille and was captured by the British fleet a few miles outside the territorial waters of Palestine on July 17, 1947. With their goal in sight, the crew and passengers fought their attackers but were unarmed and did not stand a chance against the British forces. Severely damaged, the *Exodus 47* was towed into the harbor of Haifa. The passengers were forced onto military transport ships, which brought them to Hamburg. This instance of total disregard for the fate of the Jewish survivors and their return to the country of the perpetrators instigated protests all over the world. On August 23 and September 7 thousands of Belsen camp residents demonstrated against the forced return of the refugees to Germany.

The British interned the returnees in the transit camps Pöppendorf and Am Stau near Lübeck, which were initially surrounded by barbed wire and tightly guarded. At both accommodations, comprised of corrugated iron huts and tents, the facilities were thoroughly inadequate, especially with winter approaching. The choice of these quarters and the shortage of supplies suggested that the British wanted to retaliate for the upheaval the refugees had caused. Nonetheless, they recognized them as DPs contrary to their previous practice. Some sought refuge in Belsen, while others boarded another illegal ship and reached Palestine before the proclamation of Israel.

On the one hand, the British actions, especially the forced return of Holocaust survivors to Germany, embittered all Jewish DPs; they became more aware than ever that rapid emigration from the camps to Palestine was unlikely. On the other

hand, pragmatic improvements occurred in relations with the British in 1947 in
Belsen. In May Rosensaft and representatives of the British military government
met and agreed that the camp population should not increase any further.
Rosensaft promised to compile accurate statistics of the camp residents.
In return, the British promised to distribute rations to all the "illegal" residents.
They also recognized the Jewish Committee as the official representative of the
Jewish DPs at Belsen; they refused, however, to recognize the Central Commit-
tee (which was comprised of the same members) as the sole representative of
all Jews in the British Zone. As a consequence, the British withheld support for
the second congress of the Central Committee in Belsen and Bad Harzburg in
July 1947. Rosensaft had requested meeting facilities, additional food rations,
extra gasoline for the foreign visitors, and the presence of the military police.

The Second Congress

The second congress marked the first democratic elections for the Central
Committee of Liberated Jews in the British Zone. The committee had existed
since September 1945 as the first self-appointed representative body for all
Jewish survivors in the British Zone. A council formed at the congress was
instructed to represent all Jewish communities and camp committees in the
British Zone. The involvement of the Jewish communities, whose representa-
tives as members of the council wielded direct influence over the Central
Committee, was one of the most important things that distinguished it from the
Central Committee of the American Zone. In the British Occupied Zone of
Germany, the DPs, and especially the Central Committee, were deeply involved
in setting up religious communities. From the outset, close cooperation was
envisioned and implemented between DPs and German Jews.

Josef Rosensaft, who was an unifying force in this meritorious and defining joint
effort, and the vice president of the central committee of the British Zone Norbert
Wollheim contacted the surviving German Jews, recruited them to help establish
state associations of religious communities, and ultimately became driving forces
behind the Central Council of Jews in Germany, which was established in Frankfurt
on July 19, 1950. In addition from the Bavarian state commissioners for victims of
racial, religious and political persecution Philipp Auerbach and Heinz Galinski,
who was liberated from Belsen and later chaired Berlin's Jewish community and
the central council for many years, Rosensaft and Wollhaft served on the first
directorate of the Central Council of Jews in Germany. Together, they laid the
foundation for the future organization of Jewish institutions in Germany. At the
start of this important mission, they had to overcome the many obstacles that
prevented surviving German Jews and DPs from joining forces in the American
Zone until the 1950s. The Central Committee in the British Zone managed to break
out of ghetto life in the DP camps and build structures with their peers living
outside the camp (who were often German survivors) that exist to this day.

Another important theme at the congress in July 1947 was the widespread accusation that Jews were trading on the black market. Of course they participated in black market activities, as did Germans and the military personnel as well but this rumor was closely related to the latent antisemitism in post-war Germany. The Jewish DPs were repeatedly suspected of trading cigarettes, coffee, tea, and other food products. This marked the revival of the antisemitic prejudice that Jews were involved in usury and bargained over prices.

After several raids, even the British were surprised at how meager the share of black market goods was in Belsen. Most of the business consisted of exchanges that enabled the DPs to trade their extra rations for urgently needed objects. Although the German population was actively involved in this trade, envy of the better supplies among the survivors merely worsened antisemitic prejudices. Without investigating their cause and effect, the press capitalized on such stereotypes and stirred up the general dislike of the DPs. Vandalism of Jewish cemeteries increased. This mood heightened fears among the survivors that without the presence of the military government, they would suffer violent attacks from the German population. The only recourse was to leave the land of the perpetrators as quickly as possible.

Establishment of a Jewish Homeland in Palestine

Political circumstances in Palestine and the restrictive immigration laws in all other potential immigration countries thwarted this effort. The Jews in Belsen were therefore overjoyed when Colonel Robert Solomon obtained 200 immigration certificates to Palestine for children at Belsen in the spring of 1946. One year later, on April 1, 1947, the first group of 395 DPs – men, women and children – left Belsen for Palestine under the British Operation Grand National emigration program. The plan was to issue 300 Palestine certificates a month exclusively to DPs from the British Zone.[26] After returning the Palestine Mandate in February and acknowledging for the first time a direct link between the fate of the survivors enduring in Europe and the establishment of a Jewish homeland in Palestine, the British intended to favor Jews from DP camps in their zone – and those from Belsen in particular – for emigration. Immigration to Palestine remained subject to restrictions. Only with the victory of the Israeli war of independence, which followed the UN Partition Plan of 1947 and the proclamation of the State of Israel in May 1948, were these restrictions lifted. From mid-February 1949 onward, groups regularly traveled by ship or airplane from the British Zone to Israel. The second transport left Camp Belsen on March 21, 1949:

In long truck convoys, over 600 people rode from Camp Bergen-Belsen to the infamous cargo platform to Bergen, where they boarded the train decked with Jewish flags... At 4:00 PM, when the train departed from the platform, over 600 people sang Hatikvah, with all their hearts and with fervor for being on German soil for the last time at the site where only a few years ago thousands of scantily clad people condemned to die were dragged from cattle cars and driven like animals to the death camp at Belsen.[27]

On 10 July 1950 the last few thousand inhabitants (including Josef Rosensaft, who immigrated to the United States with his family) left the camp at Belsen, which then closed its gates. Rosensaft's decision not to fulfill the Zionist ideal of immigrating to Israel was emulated by most Central Committee members. Conversely, most Central Committee officials in the American Zone did go to Palestine and Israel, possibly because they had left earlier and were consequently less influenced by the reports of the difficult conditions in the Near East. Nor were many alternatives available at the time: immigration to the United States became an option only with the liberalization of American immigration laws in 1948 and 1950.

By 1951 all Jewish DPs who were willing and physically able to emigrate had left Germany. In 1952 all remaining DPs throughout the Federal Republic were transferred to Föhrenwald at Wolfratshausen, located 25 kilometers south of Munich and the only Jewish DP camp still in operation. The final chapter in the Jewish DP history in Germany ended on February 28, 1957, when the last inhabitants left Föhrenwald.

Kindergarten

Breakfast in the Kindergarten.
Right: Zippy Orlin.

גן ילדים

KINDERGARTEN

Sala Yassy teaches young children gymnastics in the Belsen kindergarten.

Playground.

The UNRRA camp bus brings the children to the Kindergarten.

"Sturdy little toddlers romped and played in the flower-covered fields, and expressed the childish emotions so long suppressed."

Childcare workers, teachers and children from the R.B. 7 children's home. Zippy Orlin, standing in the back row, second from the right.

"From every corner of war-torn Europe were brought the orphans."

Staff of Bergen-Belsen children's home helps feed a group of young orphans.

Jewish DP patients at the Glyn
Hughes Hospital in Belsen.

DP children of the Housing Unit
R.B. 7. *"Their impressionable
minds slowly began to react to
the kind treatment and within a
few months the children of R.B. 7
were molded into one happy
family."*

Teachers. *"When the lively throng
of children had left the teachers
had time to relax."*

*"Self [Zippy], Kurt and Larry in
Canteen 5, June 5th 1947."*

Survivors worked half days as teachers and childcare workers. They wore white uniforms. Right, wearing an AJDC uniform. Hilde Jacobstahl.

A nurse at the Glyn Hughes Hospital, January 1, 1947.

Zippy Orlin.

Social Life in the Jewish DP camp at Bergen-Belsen

Thomas Rahe

Barely two kilometers from the former concentration camp Bergen-Belsen, in the barracks of the Bergen-Hohne military training grounds in Celle, the largest Jewish community in Northern Germany (except for Hamburg) emerged in the spring of 1945: the Jewish DP Camp Bergen-Belsen. It had its origins in Camp II of the concentration camp, which the SS camp administration had set up in a section of the barracks complex.

This Jewish community was most unusual and bore no legal or organizational resemblance to any that had existed in Germany before the Holocaust, nor to those formed in many cities following the liberation. The Bergen-Belsen Jewish DP camp, which existed until July 1950, was more of a political-social Jewish community than a Jewish religious community. It was an extraterritorial enclave from which German law and order and administrative authorities were excluded. Instead, the British military government had jurisdiction there.

This Jewish community had hardly any German Jews; it consisted almost entirely of East European Jews of various nationalities – somewhat like a *shtetl* transferred to the Lüneberg heath. Set up as a transit community, the intention was to close it as soon as possible.

Bergen Belsen was liberated by the British Second Army on April 15, 1945. Within a few days of the liberation, a committee was formed in Camp II to represent the interests of the liberated Jews. Josef Rosensaft was soon appointed its spokesman. In late September 1945 a Central Committee of Liberated Jews was elected in the British Zone, which was based at the Bergen-Belsen DP camp. Not only did the liberated aim to be self-sufficient from the outset, they also longed for recognition as a specifically Jewish national group over the resistance of the British military government and did not want to be repatriated to their respective countries of origin in Eastern Europe. Their chief political objective was to enable all Jewish DPs to emigrate to Palestine as quickly as possible, where they hoped a Jewish state would soon be proclaimed.

The Bergen-Belsen DP camp was therefore not intrinsically a Jewish community but was structured and legitimized by its specific functions and missions. It was primarily a site and facility for individual and collective physical, emotional, and social rehabilitation, restoration of independence and self-sufficiency, with a view toward building a new life that the Jewish DPs could imagine only outside Germany, and in most cases only within a Jewish state in Palestine.

Whether, when, and how this new start might be accomplished depended on political circumstances, and made life in general at the Bergen-Belsen Jewish DP camp highly politicized. For the time being the Jewish DPs were at the mercy of international politics. They tried zealously to influence the political course of events. The paramount importance of political involvement at the Bergen-Belsen DP camp arose from the desire of the Jewish DPs to transform themselves from objects of history (their experience during the Holocaust) to actors in their own history. Political activism was part of their collective rehabilitation.

Zionism was the focus of this political activism. Most of those who believed their future was in the United States or other traditional immigration countries also viewed Zionism as a basis for forming communities. In addition to being a grounds for political consensus, Zionism was a political ideology: it provided a historical-political definition of Judaism and a plausible interpretation for the most recent Jewish past (and of personal experiences of persecution during the Holocaust). Accordingly, Zionism also gave a sense of purpose to those who had lost their religious faith as a result of the Holocaust experience. It defined political activism and figured in all aspects of life in the Jewish DP camp, from schooling for the children through cultural activities to the organization of social life.

The two main events in the lives of the Jewish DPs – the liberation in the spring of 1945 and the establishment of the State of Israel in May 1948 – were also essential in the history of the Bergen-Belsen DP camp. In addition to being milestones in military and political history, they were viewed as part of a social and political process. The Jewish DPs initiated the process of establishing a Jewish state in their own surroundings by founding pseudo-governmental institutions, such as the Central Committee of Liberated Jews in the British Zone (as the "government" of the Jewish DP camp), their own police force and a camp court of law, schools, vocational training institutes, political parties, and the like. These institutions also helped prepare them for their future in the Jewish State of Israel, especially considering the abundance of Hebrew courses and vocational training. In this respect, the Bergen-Belsen Jewish DP camp was more a *hachshara* (Zionist preparatory training camp) than a typical Jewish community.

"Boys gather wood."

Composition of Bergen-Belsen

From the late fall of 1945, two general groups of former inmates remained at Bergen-Belsen: non-Jewish Poles and East European Jews. In November 1945 the camp population was comprised of around 16,000 DPs, of whom 11,000 were predominantly Polish, Hungarian, or Romanian Jews. At this point it was a Jewish DP camp in only a limited sense, since the British refused to acknowledge an authentic Jewish status for the Jews among the DPs or to recognize their elected representative bodies.

In the long run the British were unable to continue this policy. From October 1945 on, Jewish DPs were assigned separate accommodations within the DP camp. By early summer of 1946, the constant conflicts between non-Jewish Poles and Jewish DPs led the British to transfer the Polish DPs to a different camp.[2] Following heated political discussions, the Central Committee of Liberated Jews in the British Zone achieved *de facto* recognition by the British.

Another factor that intensified conflict between the Jews who ran the DP camp and the British was the issue of "infiltrees." These were Jews from Eastern Europe who had not lived inside the Reich during the Holocaust and had been liberated away from their former home. They only arrived later in the area, as refugees in the Western zones of occupation. Most were Polish Jews who had fled the postwar anti-Semitism in Poland (especially following the Kielce pogrom in July 1946) to seek refuge in the DP camps in the Western zones of occupation and in the American Zone in particular.

While the British military government could not completely ban these Jewish refugees from the British Zone, it refused to recognize them (unlike the Ameri-

can military government) as DPs, and thus excluded them from allocations of
food, accommodations, and clothing, and the right to enter the DP camps.
The British military government merely agreed to add some of these "illegal"
Jewish refugees to the register (provided they had reached the Bergen-Belsen
DP camp before July 1, 1946, i.e., before the Kielce pogrom). All other Jewish
"infiltrees" were treated as German refugees. In fact, their escape from Poland
and the other East European countries to the zones occupied by the Western
powers in Germany was largely organized by the *Bricha* (illegal emigration
organization). This organization's main objective, however, was the illegal transfer of Jewish DPs to Palestine, so bitterly resisted by the British. The Jewish
DP camps, their institutions and movements – in Bergen-Belsen as well – tended
to be deeply involved in these efforts. The absorption of the "illegal infiltrees,"
as well as the transfer of DPs to Palestine by the *Bricha*, needed to be kept
secret from the British. The Jewish administration of the Bergen-Belsen DP camp
therefore had reason to conceal the number of resident Jewish DPs and fluctua-
tions in their numbers.

The official statistics list the following figures for Jewish DPs at Bergen-Belsen:[3]

January 1946	9,000
June 15, 1946	9,199
August 17, 1946	11,139
February 22, 1947	10,867
August 15, 1947	8,810
November 30, 1947	8,311
December 31, 1947	7,877
April 30, 1948	8,124
October 28, 1948	6,870
March 1949	4,679

These figures are deceptive, however. On the one hand, they reflect the prevailing practice of Jewish camp DP administrations not to report the departure of
DPs who no longer lived in the DP camp for various reasons – including death,
transfer to another DP camp (often in search of family members), possibly illegal
immigration to Palestine – to the British or UNRRA (United Nations Relief and
Rehabilitation Administration). Thus they continued to appear in the register and
were included in the statistics. This practice, which appears to have been more
successful at Bergen-Belsen than at other Jewish DP camps, served to maxi-
mize the allocation of food and clothing, based on the number of registered DPs.
This ensured adequate material conditions for accommodating the Jewish
"infiltrees" that resided in the Bergen-Belsen DP camp, without the British
knowing either their names or their exact number; they were unregistered and
excluded from the allocations. On the other hand, the official statistics did not
reflect these "illegal infiltrees," who were estimated by the UNRRA (as well as by

the British military government) to amount to at least 1,500 by November 1946.[4]
Notwithstanding these statistical uncertainties, the population of the Bergen-
Belsen DP camp is believed to have comprised about half the Jews in the British
Zone. In addition, Bergen-Belsen was by far the largest Jewish DP camp in post-
war Germany (even though the overwhelming majority of Jewish DPs lived in the
American Zone).

The Bergen-Belsen Jewish DP camp became primarily a community of fate.
The Jewish DPs were connected through the traumatic experience of the Holocaust, which uprooted them and brought them together in a social community
of their own. It was a historically constituted Jewish community that primarily
pursued collective goals defined by Zionism and had a strong component of
internal solidarity. The camp was not free from conflict, however, nor was it
socially homogeneous. Even the experiences of persecution differed greatly.
While at first the Jewish DP population of Bergen-Belsen was comprised largely
of concentration camp survivors, Jews who had survived the Holocaust in ghet-
tos, in hiding, with the partisans, or in the Eastern territories of the Soviet Union,
soon outnumbered the camp survivors and became the majority. There were
also clear national distinctions among the concentration camp survivors: while
most Hungarian-Jewish concentration camp survivors had been interned for
only a few months, most Polish Jews had spent several years there.

In addition to population size, the social structure of the Jewish DPs in Bergen-
Belsen changed considerably over the period of the DP camp's existence.
The initial age distribution was significantly different from standard demographic
patterns. Children and youngsters, as well as the elderly, were especially likely
to die in the Holocaust and were heavily underrepresented.[5] Most Jewish DPs
had lost their entire family or at least most of their relatives in the Holocaust.
In the spring of 1946, however, the repatriation of East European Jews who had
survived the Holocaust in the Soviet Union brought more Jewish families with
children, as well as older Jews, to the DP camp near Bergen-Belsen.

The composition also changed significantly with respect to countries of origin.
In the summer of 1945 Polish Jews accounted for about half the Jewish DPs at
Bergen-Belsen, but their numbers increased noticeably in the course of 1946.
By November 1946 about 7,900 of the 10,600 Jewish DPs officially registered
at Bergen-Belsen came from Poland, 1,400 from Romania and 1,100 from
Hungary.[6]

Bergen-Belsen Social Life

Faced with the trauma of having lost most or all of their family members in the
Holocaust, many Jewish DPs tried to reestablish their social lives by starting
a new family. By early June 1947, a total of 1,438 marriages had taken place
at the Bergen-Belsen DP camp.[7] Most of these marriages were performed
according to traditional Jewish ritual. Those who had previously been married

had to present incontestable evidence that their former spouse was no longer alive. Considering the reality of the Holocaust, this requirement was often exceedingly difficult to fulfill, both for the concerned parties and for the rabbis at the DP camp.

In addition to the many marriages, the very high birth rates attest to the unusual social circumstances within the Jewish DP camp. By 1947 about 15 babies were born each week, and the birth of the thousandth baby at Bergen-Belsen was celebrated in early February 1948. These babys not only embodies the desire of their parents for new social support through creating a family of their own, they were also interpreted by the mothers as evidence of their own fertility. Many women who had survived the Holocaust in concentration camps feared that the deprivations and abuse they suffered had left them infertile. One problem was that several female DPs who had survived the Nazi concentration camps still suffered from the physical effects of their imprisonment and became pregnant before they had fully recovered their health.

The multitude of marriages and births also led to changes in the social and the demographic structures of the Jewish population in the camp. Jewish relief organizations and the Jewish self-government were forced to deal with new social demands, ranging from allocation of housing for new families to medical care for pregnant women and newborn babies to the need to open a kinder-garten.

The presence of Jewish children at the site of a former concentration camp was highly symbolic, not only for the newly formed families at Bergen-Belsen. Many DPs regarded these children as living proof of the collective will to survive and the vitality of the *sheerit hapleita* (the remainder of those rescued), as the Jewish Holocaust survivors called themselves. The paramount importance of childcare at the Bergen-Belsen DP camp was, therefore, hardly surprising.

Educational Arrangements

Raising and educating children and young adults was extraordinarily difficult for more reasons than the initial lack of instructional materials and professional teaching staff. Many of the children were severely traumatized by the Nazi persecution and had to relearn or discover normal social interaction skills. Children of the same age differed considerably with respect to their prior educa-tional experiences and their native languages. Most of the instruction was in Yiddish, while other languages such as Polish or Hungarian were used wherever necessary. Given these difficult conditions, the ability of the DPs to initiate and manage the entire educational system at Bergen-Belsen almost independently was quite remarkable.

The elementary and junior high school opened in September 1945, and the Jewish gymnasium (college preparatory secondary school) in December 1945. There were also a few religious schools and a rabbinical seminary. Most of the teachers were Jewish DPs themselves and received support from some members of the Jewish Brigade and delegates from Palestine. In addition to the usual subjects, Hebrew and the geography and history of Palestine received special emphasis, which was another expression of the Zionist orientation of the education.[8]

The orphans required special care. From early 1946, they were housed at the Warburg family estate in Hamburg-Blankenese, where the children prepared for *aliyah (emigration to Palestine)*. A smaller orphanage was also opened in Lüneberg.

A vocational training program for teens and some adult DPs without any occupational training was opened in 1947; it was comprised of various vocational schools and had an enrollment of about 1,500.[9] The instruction was primarily in trades involving manual labor. The lack of raw materials, however, prevented most DPs from practicing the occupation they learned at the DP camp. Nearly all the Jewish DPs at Bergen-Belsen refused to participate in the economic restoration of Germany. Social and economic interactions with the German population occurred only sporadically. A small minority of the Jewish DPs (altogether about 1,000) obtained employment at the Bergen-Belsen DP camp with the British military government, the UNRRA, or later the IRO (International Refugee Organization), or a Jewish relief organization.

The Camp Economy

Economically, most DPs were dependent on handouts from the British army or UNRRA as well as on supplies from the Jewish relief organizations. Into the winter of 1946/47, goods required for daily subsistence (especially clothing and perishable foods) were in short supply at the DP camp. There were insufficient dairy products available to nourish the growing number of babies. The precarious housing facilities were another problem at the DP camp. Most of the accommodations were overcrowded. At the end of 1945 some rooms had 10 people living in them. Privacy was virtually non-existent. Only families were assigned a room of their own. All kitchens and bathrooms were community facilities.[10]

Aid deliveries from Jewish organizations, which included religious ritual items, food supplies, and clothing, enabled the Jewish DPs at Bergen-Belsen to provide the "infiltrees" and the Jewish refugees smuggled out of Eastern Europe with help from the *Bricha* en route to Palestine. This aid also promoted Jewish solidarity and furthered the establishment of the Jewish state in the process. The aid deliveries also enabled them to trade on the black market, like the majority of Germans until the currency reform. Since the DPs received goods (especially food products) from the relief organizations rather than cash, the black market was the only way for many DPs to obtain household supplies or furnishings.

The Jewish camp administration was entirely reliant on the material support and outside professional assistance for the many social services. Basic care for the DPs at Bergen-Belsen was the responsibility of the British Army from the outset, and of the UNRRA from early March 1946. At first the British military government prohibited contact between the Jewish relief organizations and the Jewish DPs at Bergen-Belsen. Only in late July 1945 was a team from the American Jewish Joint Distribution Committee (the Joint) permitted to start working at Bergen-Belsen. The team was assisted by staff from the Jewish Relief Unit British-Jewish Aid organization from August 1945 onward.

Other Jewish organizations followed, often with specific missions. They included the Organization for Rehabilitation Through Training (ORT), which organized occupational training and retraining at the Bergen-Belsen DP camp, as well as the Jewish Agency and the Hebrew Sheltering and Immigrant Aid Society (HIAS), which arranged *aliyah* and emigration for the Jewish DPs. The Joint was the more influential of the two relief organizations, if only because it had more staff at Bergen-Belsen. It supplied most of the material aid for the Jewish DPs and performed tasks that were of immense importance during the start-up phase of the DP camp, such as registration of Jewish DPs and the corresponding organization of a search service and a postal service. The Jewish Relief Unit devoted its initial energies to social missions such as caring for small children and pregnant women.

The Jewish relief organizations supported medical care for Jewish DPs as well. The Glyn Hughes Hospital (named after one of the British liberators of Bergen-Belsen) near the Bergen-Belsen DP camp was the central Jewish hospital for the British Zone. The large number of patients at the Glyn Hughes Hospital necessitated recruitment of non-Jewish German physicians – a practice that initially instilled great fear and resistance among many Jewish concentration camp survivors. A report from the Joint dated November 1947 read: "The hospital is staffed almost entirely by German doctors and nurses. This fact aroused considerable complaints at first; it is reported, however, that the German staff has performed its duties very satisfactorily, and the situation is now accepted by the DP population."[11]

The meeting of the Jewish survivors with British Army rabbis was of immense psychological importance. These rabbis were practically the first Jewish people they encountered following the liberation (the Jewish relief organizations became involved only much later) and from whom they received immediate support. While these individuals provided little material assistance, their immense dedication and comprehensive spiritual care were invaluable to the Jewish survivors. The same was true for the members of the Jewish Brigade, who reached the Bergen-Belsen DP camp as members of the British Army in the autumn of 1945. As strident, strong, and well-respected Jews, they were the opposite of the Jewish concentration camp inmates and thus had a major impact on the Jewish DPs by leading them to identify with the Zionist cause.

Social and Emotional Consequences

The social and emotional consequences of imprisonment in a concentration camp were very difficult to overcome, especially in a DP camp setting. At times these scars complicated communication between the Holocaust survivors or Jewish DPs and the staff from relief organizations. The French physician, H. Nersen, who arrived at Bergen-Belsen in late July 1945, noted: *Nearly all are extremely unstable, irritable and quarrelsome. Most refuse to tolerate contradictions and take any opposing view personally; they rightly feel they are very different from those who do not share their gruesome experiences and are instinctively suspicious of them. Instability seems to be almost universal in their psychological constitution. In the middle of a conversation, something trivial or even no foundation at all may send them into a fit of rage and lead them to lose all self-control and erupt in a verbal diatribe or resort to violence. These crises usually end as suddenly as they start, and memories of them appear to dissolve instantly as well. On the other hand, still being interned and surrounded by barbed wire is terribly depressing, since it gives them the terrifying, torturous feeling of still being imprisoned.*[12]

The Jewish DPs did their best to regain their self-confidence and come to terms with their own traumatic persecution experiences. In addition to the political activities, which should also be considered in this context, this process consisted primarily of cultural pursuits. The Kazet Theater (named from the abbreviation for concentration camp) was probably the most important such medium. Its first performance was in September 1945 and featured both professional artists and amateur actors. The plays, which were performed largely in Yiddish, derived in part from the tradition of Yiddish popular theater and depicted the revival of the East-European Jewish *shtetls* destroyed in the Holocaust. In addition to entertaining plays, the Kazet Theater's repertoire consisted of plays written by the members that presented starkly realistic situations portraying the Nazi persecution of the Jews and the Jewish responses. The Kazet Theater thus provided Jewish DPs with much-appreciated entertainment and served as a form of subconscious theatrical group therapy. Besides the actors and the director and manager Samy Feder, many other Jewish DPs were involved in the theater, since all stage sets and costumes were created at Bergen-Belsen.

A staff member of the Joint at Bergen-Belsen best expressed the intensity with which the DPs confronted their own past in an article published in the *New York Times*: *Most striking to American correspondents, who have witnessed a performance of the displaced persons' theater, is the stark realism and sheer drama that these ex-internees portray in their show. Scenes with flames reaching out onto the stage depicting Jews being led to the crematoria, or showing Germans crushing the skull of a child, are commonplace. What strikes home is that this is not acting, but factual reproduction of what they have endured.*

Playing soccer amid the
residential units.

*When one of the child actors pathetically sobs, "Mother, I'm hungry, I'm hungry,"
a shudder passes through the entire audience… Most striking is the audience
reaction to this type of drama. It must be borne in mind that the audience is
composed of survivors of extermination centers. At the finale there never is
applause, just significant and painful silence that hangs heavily over the theater.
It is not uncommon to see an audience of over 3,000 persons burst into tears
and hysterical sobbing throughout the production. In seeing their former
miseries acted out, their lives projected onto a stage, so to speak, the displaced
persons have come to regard their theater as something a great deal more than
"entertainment." The theater symbolizes their will to live. It represents a culture
that survived a systematic attempted extermination, and throughout the camps
the people talk with great pride of their theater… Why do people come to such
a theater while their scars are still deep? One possible answer suggests itself.
The Kazet-Theater serves a therapeutic value in providing a great emotional
release.*[13]

Publications

The DP camp inmates published extensively about their experiences as well.
In July 1945 the first issue of *Undzer Sztyme* appeared. This Yiddish camp newspaper was printed in Hebrew characters. Not intended for the general public,
it specifically addressed the Jewish displaced persons. *Undzer Sztyme*, which
was the first DP newspaper in Yiddish in post-war Germany, was published by
the Central Committee of Liberated Jews at Bergen-Belsen.

In addition to news about political events that would affect the future of the
DPs and information about Jewish life within and outside Germany, Palestine
and Zionism were leading themes. The title *Undzer Sztyme* served a programmatic purpose. The camp newspaper aimed both to inform and to give the
Jewish DPs a voice to articulate their motives, which stemmed primarily from
their traumatic experiences of persecution under the Nazi regime. In article after
article in *Undzer Sztyme*, Jewish DPs at Bergen-Belsen described these experiences and memories and explored their significance for their personal and
collective future.

The historical commission that gathered memories and testimonies of the
Nazi persecution of the Jews from the Jewish DPs served a similar purpose.
An exhibition of photographs and an accompanying catalogue were prepared
on this theme.[14] A classic manifestation of how the persecution experience
affected social life at the DP camp was the practice among Jewish DPs of calling
their DP camp Bergen-Belsen, while the British consistently referred to it as the
Hohne Camp.

The proximity of the former concentration camp site – another remarkable
feature of Bergen-Belsen – made it easier for Jewish DPs to arrange memorial
events at the historic site.

It was *Undzer Sztyme*, however, that functioned as a bulletin board for the DP camp and provided space for personal announcements. While at first these were mainly questions concerning the whereabouts of missing relatives, the number of wedding and birth announcements increased over time.

In addition to *Undzer Sztyme* as the official organ of the Central Committee, there were other periodicals. Most were issued by political parties in the DP camp and were also in Yiddish. One of the most important publications in Bergen-Belsen was the register of names of Jewish displaced persons residing there. Published in September 1945, it facilitated the search for relatives. In addition, several other periodicals and monographs appeared at Bergen-Belsen, especially about Jewish culture.[15]

Cultural Life

Besides the Kazet Theater and the several publications, there were also concerts, a library, and a movie theater, as well as organized sports. Musical performances started at the Bergen-Belsen DP camp in the summer of 1945. The musicians included both DPs and guest performers from outside the camp. In July 1945, for example, Yehudi Menuhin performed with Benjamin Britten at Bergen-Belsen.[16] The multilingual camp library opened in September 1946, and was accessible to all the Jewish DPs (books were provided by the Joint).

Another important opportunity for leisure pursuits was the movie theater at Bergen-Belsen. Most of the movies featured there were in Yiddish, English, and German. While entertainment was the primary purpose, the movies were of educational value as well. The movies in English were a source of language instruction. Radio could not serve this purpose to the same extent since the broadcasts were largely in German and English, which many DPs knew insufficiently or not at all, and could not understand them without the visual medium of the movies.

Sports were the most important leisure pursuit, however. Facilities were built and equipped for many different sports: boxing, tennis, and soccer. Several sports associations were founded, and their members competed in tournaments against other DP camps. Culture and sports were so important because many DPs had ample free time that they tried to use meaningfully.

Religious and Political Life

Religious observance varied widely among the Jewish DPs at Bergen-Belsen. All the necessary facilities for an Orthodox Jewish lifestyle were present here. These included a *mikveh (ritual bath)*, synagogue facilities, religious primary schools, and a supply of kosher food products. The efforts to observe Jewish dietary laws and the demand for kosher food products suggest that 20 percent of the DPs were strictly Orthodox.[17]

Despite the efforts of the Jewish camp administration to enable or facilitate

a Jewish-Orthodox lifestyle by establishing the material conditions and corresponding social arrangements (for example with respect to Sabbath observance
at the DP camp), serious conflicts kept arising between the religious Orthodox
(primarily Hungarian Jews) and the camp administration (where Polish Jews
dominated) or secular Zionist Jews. Ultimately, separate Orthodox organizations
arose within the DP camp which refused to work with the Central Committee.
These conflicts also concerned the priorities that should rule the political and
social actions of the Jewish administration at Bergen-Belsen DP camp.[18]

The work of the rabbis at Bergen-Belsen was equally important. They formed
a council of rabbis that comprised rabbis responsible for Jewish DPs outside
Bergen-Belsen as well. The chairman of this council was the previously liberal
Zvi Asaria (Helfgott), who was also appointed chief rabbi for the British Zone in
1947. Besides Asaria, the rabbis Chaim Maisels, Israel Moses Olevsky, Israel
Zelmanowitz, and Joel Halpern were particularly prominent.

Just as the intensity or absence of religious orientation defined the lives of
individual DPs, the strength of Zionist outlook and its influence on contemporary
daily life also varied, notwithstanding the basic Zionist consensus at the DP camp.
DPs who did not question the legitimacy of Zionism but for personal reasons
believed that their future was in the United States or other immigration countries
in the West usually opposed leftist Zionist groups, which anticipated life in a
Jewish state even before *aliyah*, and tried to practice a new Zionist-socialist
lifestyle at the Bergen-Belsen DP camp. By 1947 these groups had organized 26
blocks as a kibbutz. Their 2,760 members accounted for a quarter of all Jewish
residents in the DP camp.[19] The appeal of Zionism in the DP camp was probably
attributable to its social cohesion, which many viewed as a surrogate family
environment.

That the political, social, and religious contrasts did not seriously jeopardize
the internal solidarity at the DP camp was largely owing to charismatic leaders
such as Norbert Wollheim, who represented the German Jews on the Central
Committee of Liberated Jews in the British Zone, and especially Josef Rosensaft,
who chaired the committee. While his autocratic leadership made him somewhat controversial among the Jewish DPs, he was well respected and was the
most important representative from the Bergen-Belsen DP camp. He was also
the most influential defender of Jewish interests in the entire British Zone. In addition to his personal authority, Rosensaft exuded a self-confident belligerence and
was largely successful in his dealings with the British military government.

The Emigration

In a survey conducted in September 1945, 68.5 percent of the Jewish DPs at
Bergen-Belsen expressed the desire to emigrate to Palestine. Nine percent
mentioned the United States as their preferred emigration destination.[20] In addition to indicating the prevalence of Zionism among the Jewish DPs, this survey

outcome reflected a measure of pragmatism. In the United States and other traditional immigration countries, immigration legislation remained highly restrictive. Only a very small number of Jewish DPs could immigrate to these countries. In this context, the illegal immigration to Palestine organized by the *Bricha* was the only truly realistic emigration option for the majority of Jewish DPs until 1948.

The establishment of the State of Israel in May 1948 enabled most Jewish DPs to emigrate from Germany legally. While the British continued to restrict emigration by Jewish men of military age from the British Zone to Israel even after the proclamation of the State of Israel, they discontinued this practice in early 1949. During the months that followed, a massive *aliyah* movement was launched. Increasingly, the traditional immigration countries (especially the United States) liberalized their immigration laws as well.

The choice of emigration destination depended both on the political or Zionist views of the Jewish DPs and on very personal considerations. If they had relatives in the United States who were in a position to help them establish a new social life and career, for example, even ardent Zionists often refrained from emigration to Palestine or Israel. The modest rate of emigration prior to the establishment of the State of Israel, and especially the mass wave of immigration that started in early 1949, changed the social structure of the Jewish DP community considerably. The emigration of DPs who had previously worked at the DP camp as teachers, rabbis, nurses, or in other occupations made it harder for the remaining DPs to maintain the social infrastructure at the DP camp. Finally, in July 1950 the last Jewish DPs left Bergen-Belsen for a camp at Jever. When this camp closed in August 1951 it marked the end of the Bergen-Belsen Jewish DP camp.

Departure

Rabbi Joel Halpern (left) and Rabbi Dr. Zwi Azaria (Helfgott, head of the Rabbinate) talk to an emissary from Palestine before leaving on the first legal transport of 300 DPs from Bergen-Belsen to Palestine.

"500 Orphans prepare for a long journey. Documents must be signed, medical examinations made. The girls attend to domestic matters."

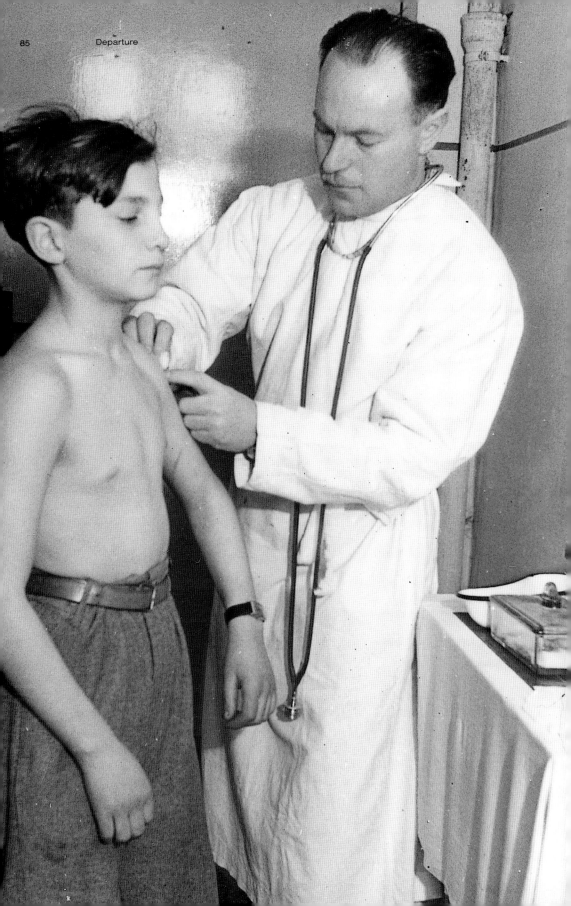

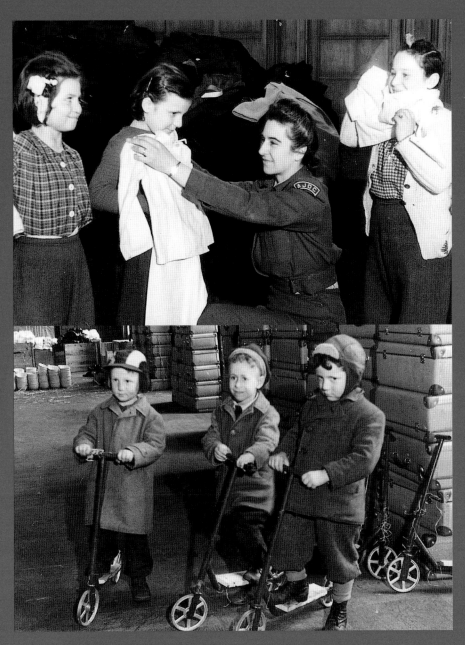

Preparing for departure.

AJDC worker Peggy Lowenthal Fink distributes new clothing to a group of girls selected to travel to Palestine.

"Suitcases are packed. Orphans left Belsen well equipped – from a pair of solid boots to a scooter."

"The farewell party at which joy and sadness mingled."

DPs, all ready to go, are brought by trucks to the train bound for Marseille, from where they will continue their journey by ship.

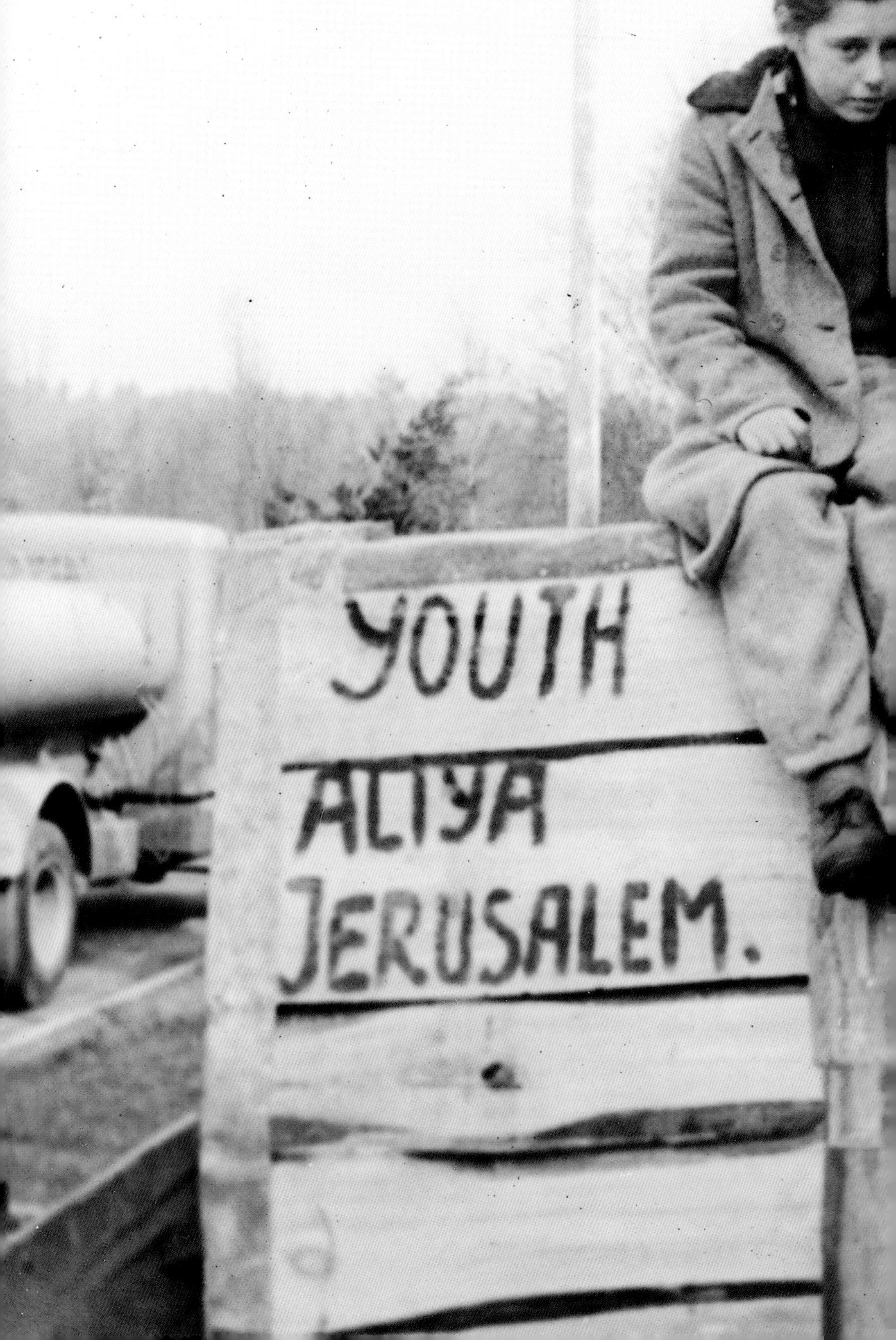
YOUTH
ALIYA
JERUSALEM.

Awaiting departure. A crate, containing baggage marked 'Youth Aliya-Jerusalem'.

"A grand send-off from their less fortunate friends, who must wait their turn."

Members of the Belsen Jewish Committee at the farewell gathering. From left to right: Clara Silbernick, Friedel Wolheim, Norbert Wolheim, Berel Laufer, Samuel Weintraub

Group photograph shortly before the departure, among them are members of the religious Zionist youth movement, Poel Mizrachi: top row, fourth from left, Sam Bloch, fourth from right: Noah Rosenfeld.

Zippy Orlin and two DP children at the departure.

A group of orphans, some carrying Purim groggers, wearing new
coats, ready to board the train to
Marseille, from where the journey
continues by ship to Palestine.

"Some of the lucky 500 orphans."

"Shalom! Shalom! Lehitra'ot!"
('Goodbye!, Goodbye!, See you later!')

"Shalom! Shalom! Lehitra'ot!"

Counselor *"Yonash the Hungarian"* among young people at their departure.

"A rabbi offers a prayer."

Saying goodbye.

"A rabbi offers a prayer, a welfare workers hugs a child and the train leaves."

The American Jewish Joint Distribution Committee and Bergen-Belsen

Sara Kadosh and Eric Nooter

Foreword

Eric Nooter was the Director of the American Jewish Joint Distribution Committee Archives in New York from 1997 until his untimely death in August 2000. One of the last projects he was working on was an essay on the AJJDC and Bergen-Belsen for publication in this volume. The following article is based on Eric's work and on source materials that he collected. It was Eric's goal to make the public more aware of the role of the Joint in caring for the remnants of European Jewry after the war. This article has been written with Eric's goal in mind. *(Eric Nooter's work appears in gray/italics in the text.[1])*   Sara Kadosh

The Holocaust forced hundreds of thousands of survivors to become displaced persons (DPs), unable or too emotionally scarred to go back to their countries of origin. The American Jewish Joint Distribution Committee, more commonly known as "Joint", or "JDC", "had to assume [much] of the responsibility for aiding the survivors ..."[2]

Since its founding in 1914, the JDC had provided assistance to Jews in need all over the world. During the 1920s, the JDC made efforts to rebuild Jewish communities and institutions in Eastern Europe that had been destroyed in the course of World War I. In the 1930s, the JDC aided Jewish refugees fleeing from Nazi Germany, Austria, and Czechoslovakia. It supported refugees en route in neutral Lisbon and Shanghai and helped them emigrate to Palestine as well as to North and South America. During World War II the JDC engaged in relief and rescue operations in Nazi-occupied countries.[3] After the war the JDC concentrated on helping the survivors.

[The JDC's] *expenditures* [totaled] *... over US$300 million between 1945 and 1950 in massive aid programs.* [It conducted programs] *in DP camps in Austria, Germany and Italy and on behalf of ... refugees from Hungary, Poland and Romania reaching the western occupation zones (often via Czechoslovakia). In the late 1940s more than 600,000 men, women and children were assisted with emigration. The JDC's decision to help finance the Brichah[4] and Aliyah Bet[5] immigration efforts enabled 115,000 refugees to reach Palestine before the declaration of the State of Israel in 1948.[6]*

JDC's involvement with Bergen-Belsen began in 1944. The camp had originally been established by the Waffen SS in April 1943 as a detention camp to hold people designated for exchange against German nationals held abroad. Very few, though, were actually exchanged. During the first year and a half, five unconnected satellite camps had been set up. The so-called 'Star camp' was the largest, containing eighteen barracks for housing Jewish prisoners, who, although not required to be dressed in the usual concentration camp uniform, had to wear the yellow Star of David, from which the camp's name was derived. Men and women lived in separate barracks but members of the same family were allowed to meet. Most prisoners were from The Netherlands ... including the JDC Holland representative Gertrude van Tijn ... Although prior to March 1944 life in Bergen-Belsen was, relatively speaking, not as bad as in other camps, by that time it had become in fact a concentration camp because of transfers of prisoners classified as ill and unfit to work. A new section was added in August to serve as a women's camp.[7]

On 15 September 1944, a JDC representative in Lisbon, Robert Pilpel, informed the JDC headquarters in New York about food parcels sent to Bergen-Belsen. He included a list of internees acknowledging receipt of the parcels by sending postcards showing barrack or block numbers and their dates of birth.

On 2 December 1944, when SS Captain Josef Kramer took over as camp commander from SS Captain Adolf Haas, Bergen-Belsen had become an official concentration camp. Thousands of Jewish prisoners from Hungary and Poland as well as prisoners evacuated from Auschwitz and Buchenwald on so-called death marches and, in 1945, thousands of male prisoners from Sachsenhausen and Buchenwald were added to the prisoners at Bergen-Belsen.

Even though it was winter there was neither adequate housing nor toilet facilities; water and food were minimal and a typhus epidemic broke out. Despite a high mortality rate, the number of inmates increased from 22,000 to more than 43,000 between 1 February and 1 April 1945.

After the liberation on 15 April 1945, the concentration camp was deliberately burned to the ground to prevent the spread of typhus and people were housed in the former German army barracks ... Within the first week of liberation, a camp committee, known as the Central Committee of Liberated Jews in the British zone, was established under the leadership of Auschwitz survivor Yossele Rosensaft, a charismatic orator, aptly dubbed the 'Abe Lincoln' of the survivors.[8]

As soon as the war was over, Joseph Schwartz [Director of European Operations for JDC] *"began to bombard SHAEF (Supreme Headquarters Allied Expeditionary Force) with repeated requests to have JDC teams brought to Germany, but to no avail."*[9]

JDC's entry into Germany was delayed because, during the first months after the war, Allied military authorities objected to the presence of civilians in the DP camps and refused to recognize that Jewish survivors were a distinct group in need of care by Jewish organizations. "The fact that the Jew on German soil constituted a special problem ... seemed to escape many in the British and American Armies responsible for the Jewish DPs."[10]

[It was not until] *1 July 1945,* [that] *Jacob Trobe, assigned by Schwartz, had arrived with the British 21st Army Group as the first JDC representative in Bergen-Belsen, in the Hanover area near the city of Celle, two and a half months after the liberation of the concentration camp by the British on 15 April.*[11]

Trobe, Eigen, and the Jewish Committee

When Trobe arrived in Belsen, he estimated there were approximately 9,000 Jewish and 3,000 non-Jewish survivors in the camp.[12] They were being cared for by the British Army, which was responsible for the Belsen camp until it was turned over to UNRRA (United Nations Relief and Rehabilitation Administration) in March 1946.

The survivors did not appear emaciated. Trobe's initial impression was that under the care of the British Army and the British Red Cross they seemed to have been "fed and clothed decently."[13] However, they were still in a weakened state, in need of extra care and nourishment. Many suffered from chronic illnesses, especially tuberculosis. Many lacked shoes, most did not have overcoats or warm clothing.

The Jewish survivors' most urgent need was to locate relatives, to communicate with them, and to join them if possible. According to Trobe, "Many do not want to migrate until they have searched all Germany and Eastern Europe for missing relatives. But this is difficult ... Lists are not ... available," and the only transport was that provided by the British Red Cross.[14]

If the DPs did have someone to correspond with in Europe or abroad, it was almost impossible for them to do so. It was illegal for DPs to write letters "in view of the restrictions on civilian mail privileges."[15] They could only fill out a form stating "I am well" or ask a soldier to send a letter for them.[16]

The survivors wanted to leave Germany as soon as possible, but few opportunities for emigration were available. Most of the survivors wanted to go to
Palestine. "One need not be a Zionist to see that Palestine has a significance for
them that is tremendous. They want to go there," Trobe wrote.[17] "I know that
if Palestine were really open to them, 80% of the people would go there."[18]

In mid-July 1945 Jacob Trobe was appointed Director of JDC Operations in
Germany, and served as director until January 1946. He opened a JDC office in
Belsen and arranged for Maurice Eigen and a team of four JDC workers to begin
work in Belsen at the end of July, even before they received official recognition
from the British Army.[19]

Within a short time, Trobe and Eigen had forged a close working relationship
with the Central Committee of Liberated Jews in the British Zone headed by
Joseph Rosensaft, as well as with British military authorities.[20] Trobe had
already reported on July 5, "I ... have organized an office of the camp Jewish
Committee ... to handle search for relatives, correspondence, migration, culture
problems and the like. The problem is so great that all my work must be with
this committee and they in turn with the people." When Eigen took over, he
helped strengthen the committee as an independent organization, despite
efforts by the British to use the JDC to weaken its status.[21] He even provided
the committee with operating expenses, although it was illegal to give money to
DPs. Trobe and Eigen's sympathy for the survivors' Zionist aspirations – as well
as Eigen's ability to speak Yiddish – also contributed to their close relationship
with the committee.[22]

Eigen's first objectives were to improve the search and location service,
organize a mail system, and establish an emigration department. The Central
Committee had tried to set up some of these services on its own, thereby duplicating the work of the British Red Cross. However, the Jews had "little faith in
the many letters and messages sent through the Red Cross."[23] Eigen coordi-
nated the work so that communications for all Jews would be centered in the
JDC office. As a result of his efforts, the British Army allowed DPs to send letters
through the JDC office in Belsen. The letters were mailed to JDC offices abroad
and forwarded to their destinations.

Welfare Activities

Eigen and his team were aided by members of the Jewish Relief Unit, Jewish
civilian volunteers from Great Britain, who were stationed in Diepholz, a small
camp also in the British Zone. Through the mediation of British military authorities,
Trobe worked out an agreement with Leonard Cohen, head of the JRU, whereby
the JRU team of twelve would move to Belsen and carry out welfare activities –
care of babies, pregnant women, and recreational and leisure activities – under
the auspices of JDC, while the JDC would continue to concentrate on location
services, communication, registration, and emigration. This would be in

accordance with the policies of UNRRA which, according to Trobe, wanted to limit the activities of other Jewish organizations to educational, cultural, and religious activities, and leave the JDC to deal with relief and rehabilitation.[24] The JRU soon took over responsibility for the children's home and children's school in the camp.

By September 1945 the survivors still lacked food, clothing, and personal items such as combs , toothbrushes, books, etc. Eigen had come to Germany without supplies, to the great disappointment of the survivors, who had anticipated that the JDC would assist them from the moment of liberation. Instead, it took months until regular shipments of supplies were received, causing bitter frustration to both the survivors and the JDC staff.[25]

The most urgent need of the survivors was for food. Basic rations were provided by the British Army and later by UNRRA. However, these rations were reduced by the Army in September 1945 and reduced further by UNRRA in 1946.[26] Moreover, the food provided was monotonous, mostly starch, "heavy on bread, potatoes, soup, pieces of ugly wurst ... No fruits or vegetables ..." and prepared in an unappetizing manner.[27] Dr. Nerson, the first JDC Medical Director in Belsen, and Dr. Fritz Spanier, JDC Medical Director for the British Zone from 1946, pointed out that although the survivors appeared well-fed, they were not really healthy. The lack of fats, proteins, and vitamins left them in a weakened state, and with poor resistance.[28]

In September 1945 Trobe began organizing shipments of food from neighboring countries. "Without any fancy supply people ... without any upper echelon clearance, we have brought some supplies into Germany from Denmark, Sweden and Switzerland."[29] The first shipment reached Belsen in early October - 38 tons of cheese, butter, eggs, jam, macaroni, milk, cakes, meat, fish, soap, as well as medicines.[30] "What a great day it was at Belsen, when 'ayer' [eggs] and 'putter' [butter] ... arrived. The first fresh eggs since the day of their internment by the Nazis," Trobe wrote.[31] Rosensaft's praise was effusive. "Mr. J. Trobe ... with his great heart ... has encouraged us and has given new hope ... . Mr. M. Eigen ... has done the maximum that a Jew is able to do for his fellow Jews."[32]

By the end of December 1945 the JDC had distributed some 90 tons of supplies in Belsen, most of it food supplies.[33] In the first half of 1946 large shipments of supplies arrived - from the U.S. alone, 475 tons of food, 85 tons of clothing, 150 kg. of medicines.[34] In May 1946 the *Jewish Daily Forward* reported that the JDC had "sent five times as much [to Belsen] as all other organizations combined."[35] In the first half of 1947 the JDC sent over 718 tons of supplies to the British Zone, mostly food, 96 tons of clothing, and 79 tons of personal items.[36]

JDC food supplies augmented the 1550 calories supplied daily by the British Army. The survivors received monthly JDC packages of cigarettes, milk, sardines, sugar, flour, jam, cocoa, cheese, tea, meat, and for men, shaving soap and razor blades. The cigarettes could be bartered with the surrounding German population for other items.

JDC also provided food supplements for children, pregnant women and other individuals in need of extra nourishment. Religious Jews received kosher food through the efforts of JDC and other voluntary agencies.[37]All the survivors received additional supplies of food and special holiday products for the Passover holidays and the Jewish New Year.

In the fall of 1945, with the approach of winter, the problem of the lack of clothing became more acute. On November 10 Trobe wrote, "People are cold (no fuel to speak of), no shoes, or warm clothing for winter … These flabby, superficially healthy people may be hit easily in any epidemic." In an effort to solve the problem, Trobe met with Judge Simon Rifkind, the newly-appointed Advisor on Jewish Affairs to the U.S. Army in Germany, to develop a "plan for JDC to buy clothing."[38] He wanted, if possible, to purchase U.S. Army clothing.[39] In an attempt to arouse American and British public opinion, Trobe leaked stories to the press about the shortage of food and clothing at Belsen and phoned Sidney Silverman, Member of Parliament and head of the World Jewish Congress in Britain.[40] "Situation is bad again, as bad as ever in Belsen," he wrote on November 20. Neither the Army nor UNRRA could meet the clothing and food needs of the DPs, he noted.[41] "JDC is doing supplementary feeding but has no clothing," he wrote in discouragement on November 21.

Finally, by the end of December, $120,000 worth of new clothing was awaiting shipment in New York, and additional shipments were planned. Soon after, 5,000 pairs of women's shoes arrived from Switzerland, enough for more than half the women in the camp.[42] Not all the clothing that reached Belsen was suitable. Some was of poor quality, the wrong size, etc.[43] These problems were gradually solved, and by mid-1946 the JDC had set up a clothing storeroom in Belsen, headed by a survivor. A 1947 report noted that used clothing was inspected to ensure its quality, and repaired if necessary. All clothing was ironed and hung on racks as in a department store.[44]

In 1946 the situation in Belsen stabilized. The British had set aside certain barracks for Jews only, and with the departure of the non-Jewish Poles in the summer of 1946, Belsen became an all-Jewish camp.[45] A JDC team of eight headed by David Wodlinger, Eigen's successor, was augmented by a group of volunteers from South Africa.[46] Wodlinger expanded the Search and Information Service and the medical services and reorganized the Emigration Department. He tried to establish an exact registration for all the survivors in Belsen and to improve the system of distributing supplies to Belsen and the British Zone. Under Wodlinger and his successor Sam Dallob, the JDC contributed to virtually every facet of life in Belsen, either on its own or in cooperation with other organizations.

A group of girls in the R.B. 7 children's home perform a play for *Tu B'Shvat* (15 days in the month of *Shvat* – New Year of the Trees).

... [The] *JDC worked together with Rosensaft's Central Committee, the United Nations Relief and Rehabilitation Administration (UNRRA), the British Jewish Relief Unit (JRU), the Jewish Agency for Palestine, the Organization for Rehabilitation and Training (ORT), and the Oeuvre de Secours aux Enfants (OSE). It also collaborated with Jewish chaplains and the Palestinian Jewish Brigade, both of whom were very active in the DP camps.*[47]

Educational and Cultural Activities

In the area of education the JDC provided textbooks and supplies for the elementary and high schools organized at Belsen by the DPs and the Palestine Brigade.[48] The JDC provided equipment for the vocational training courses conducted by ORT, including a lathe obtained from the Canadian Army, sewing machines, and an automobile for the automotive course. *Hachsharot* (agricultural training programs) organized by the Zionist movement outside Belsen received food and supplies from the JDC, as did the maritime training course set up by ORT near the town of Neustadt. Other courses included dressmaking, electrical engineering, carpentry, and a dental mechanics workshop.[49] In 1947 ORT had 443 students and 30 instructors in Belsen.

The JDC was especially involved in the area of child care. In 1946 the JDC organized a kindergarten in Belsen staffed by JDC personnel, one of whom was Zippy Orlin.[50]

The Bergen-Belsen kindergarten had two playrooms, which doubled as spaces where the children did exercises and had their snacks and lunch, a kitchen, a cloakroom, a room for kids who were sick, and an open-air playground. Some 70 children, aged 3 to 6, were picked up by bus. Schooldays started at 10:15 a.m. with exercises followed by a snack, outdoor or indoor play depending on the weather, lunch at noon, a nap between 1:00 and 2:30 p.m, drawing, etc., tea and bread before being brought back by bus around 4 p.m.

A nursery was also established at Belsen but it was soon converted into a children's home.[51] By June 1947 it had facilities for 50 children, and was staffed by five DP teachers and group leaders, a JDC medical officer, and a DP nurse. JDC provided clothing and extra food for the children in Belsen, and also supported the Luneburg children's home, an orthodox institution with 35 children outside Belsen.

In January 1946 the JDC opened a children's home for forty orphans in Blankenese on the estate of Max Warburg overlooking the Elbe River. Warburg was a member of the JDC board of directors. The estate had been confiscated by the Nazis when the family fled Germany in 1938 and was returned by Allied troops after the war. Selma Bendremer, an American social worker, now Sally Wideroff, had been assigned by the JDC to prepare the mansion as a children's home and school. [52]

The children in the Warburg home ranged in age from five to twenty, but most were between twelve and eighteen years old. Wideroff identified the children as coming from Poland, Hungary, Romania, Czechoslovakia and other countries. The first teachers were recruited from among the DPs and also among soldiers from the Palestinian Jewish Brigade.

The first teachers were recruited from among the DPs as well as from the soldiers of the Palestinian Jewish Brigade. In April 1946 105 orphans left for Palestine. During the following year the Warburg home in Blankenese continued to house orphans from Belsen and from the British Zone. JDC provided supplemental rations for the children and paid for repairs and maintenance of the home. Approximately 70 children left for Palestine in the spring of 1947 as part of the British Grand National program. The JDC outfitted each child with shoes, clothing, underwear, and a towel. The children spent two weeks at the Bocholt transit camp, then proceeded to Marseilles to board the ship for Palestine.[53]

After the departure of this group, additional children arrived at Blankenese from the American Zone. They were smuggled into the British Zone, since it was now easier to obtain certificates for Palestine for children in the British Zone than in the American Zone. The children were sent first to the children's home at Belsen, and from there were transferred to Blankenese.

The JDC directed and maintained the children's home at Blankenese, while the educational program there was organized by representatives of the Jewish

Agency. Classes in Hebrew and other subjects were held in the mornings, with the emphasis on outdoor sports in the afternoons. The home had a kosher kitchen, and religious services were conducted on Friday evenings and Saturday mornings. Groups of children remained in the home for about two months, until their departure for Palestine. In 1948 the children's home at Blankenese became a Nutrition and Health Center for Jewish children from the British Zone. The home was closed in 1949.[54]

The JDC supported cultural activities in Belsen for adults as well as for children. JDC purchased a printing press for *Unser Sztyme*, the Belsen newspaper, and subsidized the tour of the Yiddish actor Herman Yablakoff in 1947. JDC imported films, including Yiddish ones, to Belsen, and for the benefit of survivors who lived outside the camp sent an old ambulance fitted out as "a mobile cinema unit, complete with a team of projectionists ... throughout the British Zone."[55] In 1946 the JDC organized a library in Belsen, set up a reading room, and provided thousands of books in cooperation with other organizations. JDC also provided tennis rackets, boxing gloves, ping-pong paddles, and other sports equipment to the many sports clubs organized by the survivors in Belsen.[56]

The JDC also provided support for religious activities in Belsen, in cooperation with the Rabbinate of the Central Committee. JDC sent religious supplies, such as skullcaps, prayer shawls, prayer books, and texts for religious study to Belsen, and provided funds for the maintenance of the synagogues and Talmud Torahs in the camp.[57]

Jewish and Zionist themes were an integral part of the educational programs in Belsen. The children's home in Blankenese, the kindergarten as well as the Belsen schools, sponsored Hanukah parties, Purim plays, and holiday performances, and an opera with Biblical themes. When UNRRA officials objected to the emphasis on Hebrew and Zionism in the Belsen schools, Harry Viteles of the JDC defended the right of the survivors to shape the educational curriculum according to their wishes.[58]

Medical Care

A major JDC contribution was in the field of medical care.[59]

JDC medical operations in Bergen-Belsen were headed by the Dutch pediatrician Dr. Fritz Spanier, who was assisted by doctors and medical personnel from the JDC and JRU, Jewish DPs and ... German medical personnel. The hospital performed regular X-ray check-ups for suspected TB patients. There was a dental clinic and JDC-supported dental program run by ORT. To accompany the many new births other pediatricians needed to be recruited. Nurses assisted early childhood educators in the Bergen-Belsen kindergarten, ensuring health care. A JDC doctor did regular check-ups of all school-age children.

In early 1947 the JDC opened a sanatorium in Merano (Italy) with a staff of fifteen physicians and nurses under Dr. Sydney Gottlieb of Johannesburg, South Africa. The Central British Fund and the Jewish communities of South Africa, South America, Canada and Australia made substantial financial contributions. Italian Public Health ministry officials collaborated with the JDC to assist ... DPs. Jewish DPs from Bergen-Belsen [were sent to Merano and] were also sent to Davos (Switzerland) to recuperate at a sanatorium operated by OSE and supervised and subsidized by the JDC.

In 1946 the JDC opened a pharmacy in Belsen stocked with modern drugs. The pharmacy filled some 3,000 prescriptions per month. JDC also provided major support for the Glyn Hughes Hospital, located near Belsen. Glyn Hughes was operated first by the British Army, then by UNRRA. When UNRRA was dissolved in the summer of 1947, the JRU took over administration of the hospital. It was then administered by JDC until its closure in 1951. JDC provided some of the staff and equipment, and supplemented the minimal allocations of supplies, medication, and food provided by the British authorities.[60] In addition to the hospital, JDC supported a convalescent home in Bad Harzburg, administered by the JRU.

Glyn Hughes remained a Jewish hospital despite repeated efforts by the British, beginning in 1947, to turn it over to local German authorities. Rosensaft protested vehemently against this move, arguing that Holocaust survivors could not be placed in a German institution under German supervision. The JDC supported his position. When the Jews still remaining in Belsen were transferred to a camp at Jever in the summer of 1950, the hospital was transferred there as well. With the closing of the Jever camp in August 1951, the hospital was finally closed.

Emigration

One of JDC's most important contributions in Belsen was in the area of emigration. During the first years of the DP camp's existence, few opportunities to leave Germany were available. The British granted only 500 certificates per month for Palestine for all the survivors in Germany. Visas to the U.S. were issued mainly in the American Zone. The JDC made great efforts to find alternative emigration possibilities. Sweden had accepted several thousand survivors for medical treatment during the last months of the war and shortly after the war had ended. When their relatives wanted to join them, JDC-Belsen processed the requests and similar requests from other zones in Germany. The JDC-Belsen Emigration Department arranged for survivors to go to France, South America, Australia, Great Britain, the U.S., and other countries. But the numbers of these emigrants was relatively small. In 1946, 535 migrated to Sweden, 984 to France, and 73 to the British Isles. In 1947, 126 migrated to European countries, including 48 to

Norway and 30 to Sweden, 67 to South America, and 24 to other parts of world.[61]

Most of the DPs in Belsen wanted to emigrate to Palestine. With no legal solution available, JDC-Belsen cooperated tacitly with "illegal" solutions implemented by the Zionist organizations in cooperation with the Central Committee. In 1946 "infiltrees" from Poland entered the British and American Zones as part of the *Brichah* movement – the semi-legal flight of Jews from Poland to Germany, seeking to escape from the anti-Semitic atmosphere in Poland and reach Palestine. The JDC helped the *Brichah* logistically and also negotiated with the Czech and American governments to keep the borders open.[62] In the American Zone the infiltrees were granted DP status and could receive assistance from UNRRA. The British, however, refused to grant them DP status. They were classified as refugees, received reduced rations provided by the German government, and were not eligible for assistance from UNRRA.

The infiltrees arrived in the British Zone in "a shockingly bad state," they needed clothing, food, shelter, and medical care.[63] JDC-Belsen immediately sent emergency assistance to groups of infiltrees wherever they entered the Zone. Some were placed in villages and towns. Others entered Belsen as "illegals." Since they could not be registered officially in Belsen, they did not qualify for DP rations and had to share the meager rations of the legal inhabitants. By August 1946 the number of Jews in Belsen had increased to approximately 11,000.[64]

JDC-Belsen provided the infiltrees in German towns with beds, mattresses, towels, kitchenware, shoes, clothing, and supplementary food. In Belsen, the Central Committee provided the infiltrees with the ration cards of those who had died or left the camp. For this reason Rosensaft consistently resisted efforts to conduct an exact registration of the residents of the camp. Despite Rosensaft's efforts, however, the additional numbers of people in Belsen resulted in reduced rations for all the survivors in the camp. JDC, which was aware of the problem, sent supplies to Belsen for larger numbers of people than were officially registered. The additional rations were also intended to compensate for the fact that the official DP rations in the British Zone were much lower than in the American Zone.[65]

In the spring of 1947 the British announced the Grand National program, whereby 350 certificates a month would be issued to the British Zone. Approximately 6,000 persons emigrated from the British Zone to Palestine as part of this program from April 1947 to May 1948.[66] JDC-Belsen conducted the medical examinations for the emigrants, outfitted the children and, when necessary, the adults, and helped organize the journey. JDC-Belsen also sent supplementary food to the Bocholt transit camp, where the emigrants had to spend days or weeks waiting to depart.[67]

JDC's sympathy with the Zionist aspirations of the DPs was clearly demonstrated in its support for the passengers of the *Exodus 1947*. The illegal immigration ship bound for Palestine was intercepted by the British, its passengers were returned to France on three prison ships, and, after nearly a month, sent back to Germany. During the time the prison ships were anchored off the coast of France, JDC sent food and other desperately needed supplies to the people on board.[68]

The prison ships docked at Hamburg on September 8 and 9. The 4200 passengers of the *Exodus* were placed in two camps in the British Zone – Am Stau and Poppendorf – both in poor condition and unsuited for occupancy in winter. After long negotiations with British authorities, JDC-Belsen succeeded in entering the camps on September 13 with food and toilet items, religious books, sacramental articles for the Jewish High Holidays, and Yiddish and Hebrew books and newspapers. At the end of September, a Jewish medical team with doctors from the JDC and the JRU and nurses from the Jewish Agency entered the camps. The Jewish team was to supervise the German medical personnel supplied by the British. The JDC also sent clothing to the *Exodus* passengers, who had arrived in torn shirts and without any warm clothes. To meet the sudden emergency, JDC-Belsen emptied its warehouses in the British Zone and requested additional supplies from the American Zone.[69]

The object of the JDC operation was to see that the Exodus people were adequately fed and clothed for the long distance they had yet to travel. JDC also pressured the British to repair the camps at Emden and Sengwarden, where the Exodus passengers had been transferred in November. Subsequently, some of the Exodus passengers entered Belsen, and a few were among those transferred to Jever when the Belsen camp closed. All eventually reached Palestine.

The establishment of the State of Israel in May 1948, and the end of Israel's War of Independence in early 1949, opened the way for emigration from Belsen to Palestine. JDC-Belsen continued to conduct medical examinations for the hundreds who left every month, and helped outfit the emigrants for their journey.[70] In 1949 the JDC office was transferred from Belsen to Hamburg. JDC continued to assist the survivors after their move to Jever in July 1950 until the final closing of the Jever camp in August 1951. JDC's involvement with the DP camp Bergen-Belsen had come to an end.

Soccer team of Sport club
Hatikvah (meaning 'the hope',
national anthem of Israel)

runs through the streets of
DP camp Bergen-Belsen.

The *Hatikvah* soccer team.

The *Hagibor* (the hero) soccer team.

"An inter-zone Football match is played in Belsen."

The *Hagibor* boxing team of Bergen-Belsen.

Theatrical productions at DP camp
Bergen-Belsen. *"Uprooted actors
recapture the atmosphere of the
good old days in play and opera."*

UNRRA director Vida Kaufman and AJDC workers at a Christmas party in the British officers club in Hamburg, December 1946.

Wedding in DP camp Bergen-
Belsen.

"Hagibor Sedar, Pesach 1947".

Wedding in DP camp Bergen-
Belsen.

The task of remembering

Genya Markon

The task of remembering takes many forms. Upon its establishment in 1993, the United States Holocaust Memorial Museum (USHMM) viewed as its primary goal to teach the history of the Holocaust to those who, for the most part, had neither personal memory nor in-depth knowledge of what had transpired. The panoply of images and artifacts comprising the museum's permanent exhibition was designed as a didactic experience to ensure that the memory of the Holocaust would be embedded in the consciousness and conscience of all visitors. Almost from the day of its inauguration, however, the museum's mission expanded as it became the repository of memory itself, and this manifested itself in one form or another by visitors who had lived through the Holocaust. Many of them did not know where their loved ones had perished or where they were buried, if at all. The museum's red brick and limestone building in the heart of Washington DC became a memorial to those who died and a shrine for survivors.

As head of the photo archives of the USHMM, I joined the professionals who were laying the programmatic and administrative foundations of the museum fourteen years ago. We were soon asked to provide images for a variety of other institutions. When the museum opened its doors to the public, visitors to our department multiplied, many of them survivors. Some had seen themselves in the photographs of the permanent exhibition and simply wanted copies. Many others, though, brought with them their own family photographs. They opened their hearts and poured out their stories. Listening to them, we realized that this immersion in memory was frequently too intense for survivors to bear alone. Sharing the past with a third party, a stranger rather than family, was sometimes easier. The oral histories and the personal documentation that accompanied them proved to be a rich lode of material that we had not initially anticipated.

Because so many individuals were lost in the Holocaust, so many families torn apart, we were keenly aware that each person and each personal image that survived was important. And we quickly discovered that nothing in the course of our work could be more gratifying than helping survivors and their children come to terms with their past, if even in a very small way.

Galvanized by this knowledge and by the spontaneous contributions of the museum's visitors, my staff and I began to attend survivors' conferences, particularly those of hidden children and child survivors. At one such event, held in Florida in 1994 under the aegis of the American Gathering of Holocaust Survivors, I met Sally Bendremer Wideroff. [See page 218] A social worker born and brought up in the USA, Sally felt a life-long bond with survivors. After World War II, she joined a team sent by the American Joint Distribution Committee[1] (the Joint) to help rehabilitate survivors in the Displaced Persons camp established at Bergen-Belsen. Sally worked primarily with children who had been brought there to recuperate. The experience was to remain with her forever – along with the numerous photographs and other documents she brought home, which she willingly gave to us. After the photographs had been catalogued in our database, I thought nothing further about them – until a trip to Amsterdam some years later.

The NIOD Photo Archives and Zippy Orlin's Album

On a trip to The Netherlands in l995, I went to the Netherlands Institute for War Documentation (NIOD) to comb through their Holocaust-related archives (as I often do in countries that had been directly affected by the war) to select images to add to the museum's holdings. There I met Rene Kok, Director of the Photo Archives, who generously allowed us to duplicate over 600 photographs from their collection. We kept in touch, and a few years later he informed me of the album of Zippy Orlin, containing over a thousand images from the Displaced Persons camp of Bergen-Belsen. In order to judge whether it was worth duplicating the contents of Zippy Orlin's album for our archives, I had to return to Amsterdam to see it for myself, although I was very aware that it would be a costly and time-consuming project to copy Zippy's 1100 photographs.

Leafing through the first pages, I was immediately struck by the care with which these images had been selected. Most were candid shots of children and staff, but one was identified as "Willy, with the Leica." Willy, it seems, was deputy transport officer of the Joint, and he took many cameras on his travels. We presumed it was he who had taken many of the photographs.

The captions on each page describing the activities depicted confirm Zippy's tremendous investment of time and emotion in assembling the album. They also reflect her own personality and preoccupations, as in these examples: "Youthful appetites and beaming faces;" "Acting and singing gave expression to their

Arrival of Belsen schoolchildren at the children's holiday home in Blankenese.

regained lust for life;" "Sturdy little toddlers romped and played in the flower-covered fields and expressed the childish emotions so long suppressed." It was eminently clear, as volunteer Betty Adler Rosenstock later wrote of Zippy, that "she hadn't lost her enthusiasm, her good cheer, and her commitment to helping others in stressful, discouraging times. I felt a kinship with her: we were both young, brought up in safe English speaking communities. I admired her..." [2]

Almost every page of the album was devoted to a different topic: the children's daily life, recreation, trips, school life, health care, rehabilitation, Chanukah celebrations, concerts and theatrical performances, mothers with their new babies, preparations for and departure to Palestine, additional rehabilitation in Merano, Italy. The range was enormous, and I scanned the pages seeking familiar faces.

Then, suddenly, I found one: a small portrait of Sally Wideroff inscribed, "To Zippy from Sally in friendship." And with that the startling fact dawned on me that through people like Sally there was a good chance we could obtain more information about others who appeared in these photographs. Fortunately, Sally Wideroff was still alive and eager to meet with me again. With a color laser copy of the album in hand, I flew to see her in Boca Raton, Florida. I learned of her role in setting up the Blankenese children's home near Hamburg, and she casually mentioned that she still had the raincoat that she had worn in many of the photographs she had donated to our museum. She explained that, depending on the weather, she either wore the lining alone or the outer coat as well. Was the museum possibly interested in the raincoat, she wondered aloud? Not merely interested, I responded, but thrilled to consider it. Thus it happened that after a 50-year sojourn across continents, Sally Wideroff's raincoat came to rest in the museum's permanent collection of material objects, where it bears witness to the events depicted in Zippy Orlin's album.

During my visit Sally told me that I must get in touch with John and Alice Fink [*see page 217*]. John's excellent memory enabled him to identify many of the people depicted in the Belsen album. He gave me a list of contacts, some in Israel, others in the United States. Through him I also learned that there had been a reunion in Israel of "Blankenese children" sponsored by Reuma Schwartz Weizman, the wife of Israel's former president, Ezer Weizman. [*See page 214*]

Students of The Hebrew University of Jerusalem had interviewed the president's wife in l993,[3] at which time she described her experiences at Blankenese:

At the beginning it all seemed a strange adventure to me. I think that none of the other young women working... there was as young as I... I concentrated on teaching the children about the Land of Israel. I had, after all, completed the Teachers Institute of the Seminar of the Kibbutzim and I had brought some material with me including a flute for singing Israeli songs... They learned to sing the song of the Chanukah dreidel [top] *for the first time.*

During my next visit to Israel, I had the honor of meeting with Mrs. Weizman at the president's house, and later with a group of those who had been "Blankenese children." Discussing that emotional reunion, Mrs. Weizman said, "I think a reward like this is given to a very few in their lifetime."[4] Ultimately, however, it turned out that only a few pages of Zippy Orlin's album were devoted to the Warburg children's home at Blankenese; the majority of her photographs were of the Displaced Persons camp at Belsen.

The DP Camp

By this time it had become obvious that the subject of Displaced Persons merited further study. The museum was planning a conference on the topic, and a small exhibition was to be mounted in conjunction with the conference. The photographs could not have been more timely in benefiting the research. Questionnaires were sent to all those registered in the Benjamin and Vladka Meed Registry of Holocaust Survivors at the museum who had indicated that they had spent time in a Displaced Persons camp after the war. Members of the collections staff met in New York with those who indicated they might be potential donors to the museum. One of them was Betty Adler Rosenstock, another Joint worker who had been in Belsen. She offered the museum some 100 photographs she had saved. I immediately noticed the resemblance to the photographs in Zippy's album, and arranged to meet with Betty at the Joint offices along with Eric Nooter, Director of the AJDC Archives. Eric was engaged in a comparison of the Joint collection of Belsen photographs with those in the Zippy Orlin album. Recalling her work as a volunteer with survivors in Belsen, Betty mentioned that she had been sent there as a social worker because of her excellent command of Yiddish and Hebrew. She appears in one or two photographs in the Belsen album, and it was she who led us to Hilde and Max Goldberg.

The Goldbergs

Hilde's story was unique. Although the camera caught her in Belsen as a lovely smiling young social worker, her cheerful face and caring demeanor belie her painful story. [*See page 224*]

Hilde allowed me to interview her in her home, sharing her family history with me. This was no easy task since, despite her invitation, she was reluctant to talk about her past. Yet our meeting seemed to mark a turning point for her: it gave Hilde renewed strength, and she decided to attend the Displaced Persons conference then being planned. She was accompanied by her husband and three daughters, one of whom later wrote a memoir of her mother. Rita Goldberg writes:

I wrote this book because I had to. I'm the child of a woman who has not only survived the Holocaust, but did so heroically, and my imagination has always swarmed with second-hand memories... Some of my own adventures as a young woman arose directly out of a hunger for greater knowledge of the past... I think of this multi-stranded narrative as an exploration of the way the traumas of history affect the imaginations of the generations who come after.[5]

Through Eric Nooter's presentation at the Displaced Persons' conference, Hilde was able to find and meet some of the children who had been under her care at Belsen. One of those children was Stefa Hasson. [*See page 220*]

Stefa Hasson

I had met Stefa some years ago in the suburbs of Washington, at a conference for child survivors and hidden children. At that time she shared with me the details of her story as well as some of her photographs. Nothing at the conference, however, prepared us for the dramatic scene when Stefa Hasson identified herself in Zippy's album. Suddenly she screamed out, "That's my doll!" There in the photograph was the doll that Stefa had been given in Bergen-Belsen, sitting next to her on a chair. On another page the doll could be seen on the grass where Stefa and other children were engaged in daily exercises. Confronting these photographs for the first time, Stefa was transformed. Suddenly she was a five-year-old child again in Belsen. Memories flooded back, and the tears flowed as, for the first time since the war, she became one with her history. The picture of this doll – the beloved object upon which Stefa had bestowed her childhood affections and dreams – was the catalyst that merged her past and present. The story of her survival, bound up with the memories of her doll, would now be part of the much larger set of events depicted in Zippy's remarkable album.

In a recent conversation with Stefa, she told me how traumatic it was for her to be reunited with her mother after the war. At the museum we often hear the outlines of similar stories, but the pain they engender generally prevents our delving further. Even fifty years after the event, the wounds are hardly closed.

The Meaning of the Photographs

Photographic research is a collaborative effort. Much time is spent cataloguing images and verifying the information in the museum's photo archives department. As we honed our visual acuity, particularly for faces, it became possible for a staff member to look at a policeman in a recently acquired photo from Belsen and declare, "That's Nandor! [*See page 223*] I just interviewed him in Florida. It has to be the same person." As indeed it was.

What can we learn from the images in photographs such as this album? Should the images of those who escaped the horrors of the Holocaust serve as reminders of this catastrophic event? Or as a reminder of the renewal of life? Or both?

For survivors themselves, Elie Wiesel perhaps best sums up the import of these pictures in *One Generation After:*

Photographs are more evocative than words, any words; they are ruthless, definitive, precise. Fascinated by the memory they imprison, the survivor studies them to rediscover an image of himself he had thought extinct: his own way of saying Kaddish, with his eyes rather than his mouth.[6]

Beyond their special meaning to survivors, can the photographs help us impart to others what the Holocaust was in its multitude of ramifications? What can these images add to humanity's understanding of this event?

In 1995 psychiatrist Robert Krell, himself a child survivor, wrote: "while in history, fifty years is an eye blink; for us as individuals, fifty years is indeed a lifetime. We have lived fifty years beyond that moment, that horror of wartime Europe in which we spent our formative years... Yet, we come together to validate memory."[7]

To validate memory and to perpetuate it – herein lies the meaning of our endeavors. And in the final analysis, helping the remaining survivors with their task is not only our moral duty, it is our historic obligation

Young people

DP children and a member of
the Jewish Brigade celebrate
Hanukah.

Young DPs at the Bergen-Belsen vocational school.

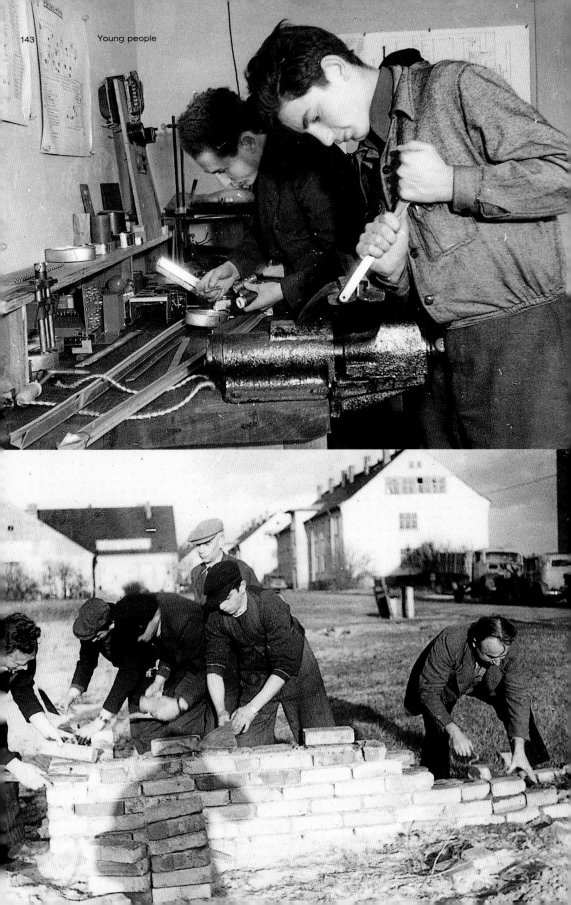

Designing and making dresses at the Bergen-Belsen vocational school.

Schoolteachers. First row, fourth from left: Dr. Michael Lubliner, school principal.

Designing and making dresses at the Bergen-Belsen vocational school.

Hanukah performance.

"Acting and singing gave expression to their regained lust for life."

"Youthful appetites and beaming faces at Oneg Shabbath."

"Can Chanukah be far away? The joy and happiness radiating from the children's faces brought happiness to all those present. Amidst singing and feasting the children were imbued with the Maccabean spirit." Hanukah, 1947.

Right wearing cap, senior Jewish chaplain of the British army and later rabbi, Sir Israel Brodie. Next to him is Josef Rosensaft (Chairman of the Central Committee of the Liberated Jews of Bergen-Belsen and the British zone) and his wife Dr. Hadassa Bimko Rosensaft (head of the Health Department).

Standing at left, Sarah Eckstein. With pipe David Kalnitzky (chief of the Jewish Police at Belsen), next to him at the rear Eva Frenkel and Dr. Sasha Gottlieb (Jewish Relief Unit).

Zippy Orlin amid DP children.

Arrival of Belsen teenagers at
the children's holiday home in
Blankenese.

Children in the Blankenese children's home pose in front of the "White House," the main building where the staff lived.

"What it's really like in a DP Camp. A South African Girl in Belsen"

Zippy Orlin

The Zionist Record, Friday, March 4, 1949
By Miss C. Orlin, who recently returned to South Africa after spending 2 1/2 years as a social worker in the Bergen Belsen Camp

The open army truck in which I was traveling to Camp Belsen bumped along the last few hundred yards of the dusty corrugated stretch of road which led to the notorious Nazi extermination center.[1] The driver, who was a former inmate of the camp, explained to me that the Jews were marched along this very road to their death. Thus, with this depressing picture in my mind, I started my work in Belsen – 27 months crammed with hard work, interesting encounters with the remnants of European Jewry, and a host of invigorating experiences. I shared their joys and sorrows, listened to the gruesome tales they had to relate, discussed their problems with them, and during the course of time became part of the life they led in Belsen.

Nearly all of the 10,000 Jews in Belsen were sole survivors or in small family groups, and at first determined at their courage at the fact that they had continued on, despite everything which made life significant. Yet their will to live was great. What kept these people alive? Some hoped that one day they would be reunited with their relatives across the seas. The majority, however, knew that ultimately they would reach Palestine, and it was always a source of considerable comfort to them to know that they were not forgotten, and that the representatives of world Jewry had come to assist them in their rehabilitation.

The original concentration camp, situated about one mile from the present camp, was burnt to the ground on April 15, 1945, when it was liberated by the

British Army.[1] All that remains is a huge cemetery where 35,000 Jews lie buried in mass graves, some of which contain as many as 5,000 bodies. A small crematorium, which was used by the Germans for burning some of the people they massacred, stands in an isolated corner at the far end of the cemetery. On April 15, 1945, the survivors were moved to what was formerly an S.S. training center. In these military barracks the people live today.

As soon as the people had recovered their health to some extent, they set about turning Belsen into an active and compact community. They set up their committees, which were responsible for the smooth functioning of the camp, for the distribution of food and clothing, and for the education of the children – in short, for the well-being of the people in every respect. The whole camp was run by the people under the guidance, and with the assistance of the voluntary agency workers from abroad.

The Belsen police force was one of the first institutions to be set up. It was 200 strong and maintained law and order for 24 hours a day, seven days a week. Police guards were placed at every exit and entrance to the camp, and they supervised all incoming and outgoing traffic.

No job was too small or too big for these men. One day, during my rounds in the camp, I lost my keycase. I had no idea in which vicinity I had dropped it but nevertheless reported the matter to the police. Within ten minutes they had gone over the camp with a fine comb and my keys were recovered. The police marched at the head of every parade, and supervised all large gatherings. The Belsen school accommodated children from six to 18 years of age. The fine staff of teachers was headed by a Doctor of Philosophy who came from Poland. Under his expert guidance the children of Belsen were given an opportunity of making up for the many years they had spent without schooling in the ghetto and concentration camps of Hitler Europe.

The teachers helped the children to regain the pleasure and the vigor of their youth and inspired them with courage and a sense of faith in the future. The great thirst for learning could never be adequately quenched. All the subjects were taught in the Hebrew medium, but the study of one other language was made compulsory. The school had a Debating Society, a Scientific Society and a theater group which put on a series of excellent plays during the course of the term. The well-equipped recreation hall was open after school hours and many socials were arranged by the students in their leisure hours. The religious school, consisting of the Talmud Torah and Yeshiva, was the center of religious life in Belsen. Groups of rabbis often stood outside the building benevolently stroking their long beards, while the chanting of the students could be heard clearly several blocks away from the school.

I often came into this institution and tried to improve the conditions under which the students lived and worked. But this was no easy task. Every few months I equipped the school with new cutlery and crockery, had the rooms

Zippy Orlin amid her co-workers
of the AJDC. From left to right:
Harry Kopp, Zippy, Margo,
Sally Wideroff, Hilde Jacobstahl,
"Dorys from South Africa,"
Egon Fink and Lotte Levinson.
In front: *"little David"*.

painted, brought in new furniture and provided new linen – but alas, no one was prepared to accept responsibility of looking after these things – all sat with their head buried deep in their books, and swayed and chanted far into the night.

The kindergarten at Belsen was an institution which could have held its own in any large city in the world. There were 100 tiny tots ranging from three to six years of age who religious attended classes each day. Here, in brightly-decorated, sunny rooms, the children romped happily at their games.

They arrived at the kindergarten at 9 a.m., did gymnastics for ten minutes, and then breakfasted. In the summer months most of their time was spent in the outdoor playground which had all the amenities of a city park. A small swimming pool was built in one corner, and here the children used to splash about to their hearts content.

After lunch they rested for some hours and were then given tea and sandwiches. At 4 p.m. the bus picked them up outside the kindergarten and dropped them at their respective "blocks." Thus the children were kept off the streets and out of their stuffy crowded rooms.

Despite this attention, the mothers were not satisfied. The Polish mothers wanted us to feed their children on herring and potatoes; the Hungarian mothers preferred "goulash" to most other dishes, and the Russian ladies insisted on cabbage soup. We managed to pacify them by giving the children a bit of everything the mothers requested, and yet managed to adhere to the diet drawn up by the camp doctors.

The Children's Home in Belsen housed 80 orphans who came from every corner of Europe. This was a wild, undisciplined crowd of youngsters who had been dragged from one country to another, from one concentration camp to another. Some had lived with Christian families since babyhood and did not know their names, who their parents were, or their country of origin. They had no faith in humanity and were suspicious of everything and everyone. They had only one desire – to get to Israel.

At mealtime they stuffed themselves hurriedly and anything that was left on the table was put into their pockets, and later hidden under their pillows. But after many months of careful and patient training they learnt that there would be more food tomorrow, and the next day, and every day until they left Belsen for Israel. They slowly began to respond to the treatment of their "Madrichim" [youth leaders], and soon the Children's Home became a lively place, full of bright-eyed youngsters going about their various duties. They took great pride in the home and decorated all the walls with pictures of life in Palestine and of the great Zionist leaders. They went to school or kindergarten – they became individuals and personalities again.

Last Step to Israel

The Ort-Oze training school at Belsen achieved wonders in the rehabilitation of many of the Jews in the camp. There were 400 students who received training in one or other of 16 occupations. To this school men and women of all ages flocked. There were morning and afternoon sessions of each course so that young and old alike were able to attend. The children came in the afternoon, while the mothers and the fathers attended the morning session.

Many who had no special training in any trade realized that some technical skill would be essential for them if they were to make a living in the country to which they emigrated. The women became dressmakers, weavers, corseteers, knitters, eiderdown makers leather workers, milliners and dentists. The men became carpenters, radio-mechanics, auto-mechanics, plumbers, fitters and turners, bricklayers, dental-mechanics and bootmakers.

The Students' Committee acted as the Liaison Office between pupil and teacher, and published a weekly magazine. The men played football, boxed and swam. The women attended gymnastic classes which I ran twice weekly in the school's recreation hall. At first these classes were not very well attended. I addressed the students several times and impressed on them the importance of exercise, particularly in view of the fact that they spent the greater part of their day in sedentary occupation. They were eventually persuaded of the benefits to be derived from gymnastics and attended the classes regularly.

The clinic was responsible for the treatment of cases of minor illness and was staffed by trained nurses and doctors, headed by AJDC personnel. The staff of the pharmacy was kept busy all day handing out pills, ointments, mixtures and bandages to the people, who delighted in the pleasant social atmosphere which prevailed at the dispensary.

Zippy Orlin in a vehicle of the
AJDC Transport Unit.

More serious cases were treated at the hospital where modern equipment
was available to deal with any emergency. The staff of the maternity section
of the hospital was kept busy all day as the birth-rate was extremely high.
The "mohels" [circumcizers] in Belsen often worked overtime.

The Cultural Department of Belsen worked in close cooperation with the
AJDC in organizing concerts and the publication of a weekly newspaper which
was printed by its own printing press. It put on plays by the Belsen Theater
Group and brought actors and musicians from other camps. It supplied the
schools with educational material, the sportsmen with equipment and the older
people with a well-stocked library which contained books in eight languages.
Sport was taken very seriously in Belsen. There were many football, ping-pong,
boxing and athletic teams, and inter-kibbutz competitions were held regularly.
Many visiting teams came to Belsen from the American Zone and were always
given a grand reception by the local sport enthusiasts.

A social worker was in charge of hospital welfare and attended to the needs
of the patients. She ran a library, distributed clothing, and organized an educational program. Some patients studied English, others did handcraft. The Ort
School sent its instructors into the hospital and the morale of the patients,
confined to bed for a long period, was maintained through the interest they
found in learning an occupation.

There were approximately 30 Chalutziut groups [pioneering youth groups] in
Belsen, the politics of these groups ranging from extreme Left to extreme Right.
There were also several religious kibbutzim. Most of the people in Belsen lived in
these kibbutzim and their representatives sat on every committee in the camp.

The president of the camp was elected by the people and carried out all negoti-ations with the army and "Occupation" authorities.

To further occupy the minds of the people in the camp every "yomtov" [Jewish holiday] was celebrated with much pomp and ceremony. Communal "seders" were held and gay "Purim" and "Chanukah" parties were thrown for the children. The school and kindergarten joined forces and put on some excel-lent plays and concerts. Dances were organized every week and parties were held for the people in the homes in which the voluntary workers lived.

Many of the people in the camp worked for the voluntary societies as filing clerks, secretaries, drivers, mechanics, cooks and waiters. Yet others were occupied in "private enterprise." For instance a tailor made suits for his friend and a dressmaker showed the ladies what they should wear. There was a ladies' hair-dressing saloon, a gent's barbershop, a manicurist and a pedicurist – and one must not forget the beautician who was a charming lady determined to practice her art on all females. I met her in the street one day and she insisted that I pay a visit to her rooms and have a "treatment," and before I could protest I was sitting on a chair, a napkin had been tied under my chin and I was being smothered in face cream. After several minutes of patting, slapping and massaging I made my escape.

The people were always extremely pleased to see the voluntary workers at the weddings and "bris melahs" [circumcisions]. I seldom missed one of these functions and enjoyed them thoroughly. They were indeed colorful affairs, for here I saw the dances of many lands, and heard the songs of Eastern and Central Europe. Hebrew songs and the "hora" [Palestinian Jewish dance of Ukrainian origin] were popular items at every social function in Belsen.

My thoughts on Belsen now are a mixture of sad and happy memories. Among the happier recollections is the effect on the camp of the declaration of Palestine as a Jewish Homeland. For a whole day and a whole night the people of Belsen danced and sang in the streets. The younger people marched around all night with flaming torches, and a meeting was held in "Freedom Square" to bless the New State of Israel. The word "Mazeltov" [best of luck] was on every lip.

The children's transport to Palestine, in March of 1948, was another memo-rable event. The Jewish Agency for Palestine was granted 500 certificates and was also to send all the orphans in the British Zone to Israel. Belsen was full of happy children preparing for the long trip to the land they had all dreamed about for so many years. It took several weeks to get the children documented, clothed and equipped for the journey. A big farewell party was organized to wish the children "bon voyage." The next day the children left. That evening I walked through the empty rooms of the home. The children had taken down pictures and pulled off the decorations. It was a strange experience not to have a mob of children following me around the house, tugging at me and chattering gaily.

And what of the sad memories? Every year on April 15, the people of Belsen

Zippy Orlin amid DP children.

would march along the dusty country road which led to the old concentration camp[2]. Here they would gather around the memorial which was built to commemorate the first year of liberation, and offer a prayer. Here lay buried the mothers, fathers, brothers and sisters of many of them. No one knew in which mass grave his dear one lay, and yet some people had put up tombstones on the graves, believing that their dear ones were buried there. After "Hatikvah" was sung the people marched back along the dusty country road, their heads lowered.

One cannot talk of Belsen without thinking of the "Exodus." In September, 1947, the "Exodus Jews" were brought to Hamburg and forced to disembark. The people in Belsen were in an ugly mood that day – a mass protest meeting was held and feelings ran high. When I visited the "Exodus" Jews at Amstau and Pappendorff they were living under shocking conditions behind barbed wire and guarded by British soldiers. But they were far from downhearted. Within a week the camp was functioning smoothly – the children were attending school, food and clothing was being distributed and babies were being born daily.

Having lived in Belsen for 27 months I cannot help but compare the Belsen I left to the Belsen I saw on my arrival in July, 1946. In 1946 Belsen was full to over-flowing with new people coming in every night – people fleeing from the anti-Jewish pogroms in Poland. Immigration was at a standstill. We managed to send out a handful of people every month, while hundreds poured in weekly. When I left Belsen towards the end of 1948 I took a completely different picture with me. Immigration on to America, Canada and Australia was on the move, but the masses were getting ready for the final stage of their long journey and the end of their suffering and humiliation – they were heading for Israel.

Special events

Press conference during the Second Congress of the Liberated Jews at DP camp Bergen-Belsen, July 20, 1947. Center, wearing glasses: David Rosenthal, editor of the Bergen-Belsen camp daily *Undzer Sztyme*.

אונדזער פליט

טראגן ליכט און קולטור

DPs wearing concentration camp uniforms march from DP camp Bergen-Belsen to the former concentration camp site for the dedication of a memorial to the 30,000 Jews who perished there, April 15, 1946.

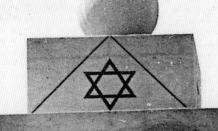

Josef Rosensaft (Chairman of the Central Committee of the Liberated Jews of Bergen-Belsen and the British zone) at the memorial service on the former camp grounds, April 15, 1946.

Following the memorial service, the gate to the concentration camp grounds is closed.

One of the mass graves on the grounds of the former concentration camp.

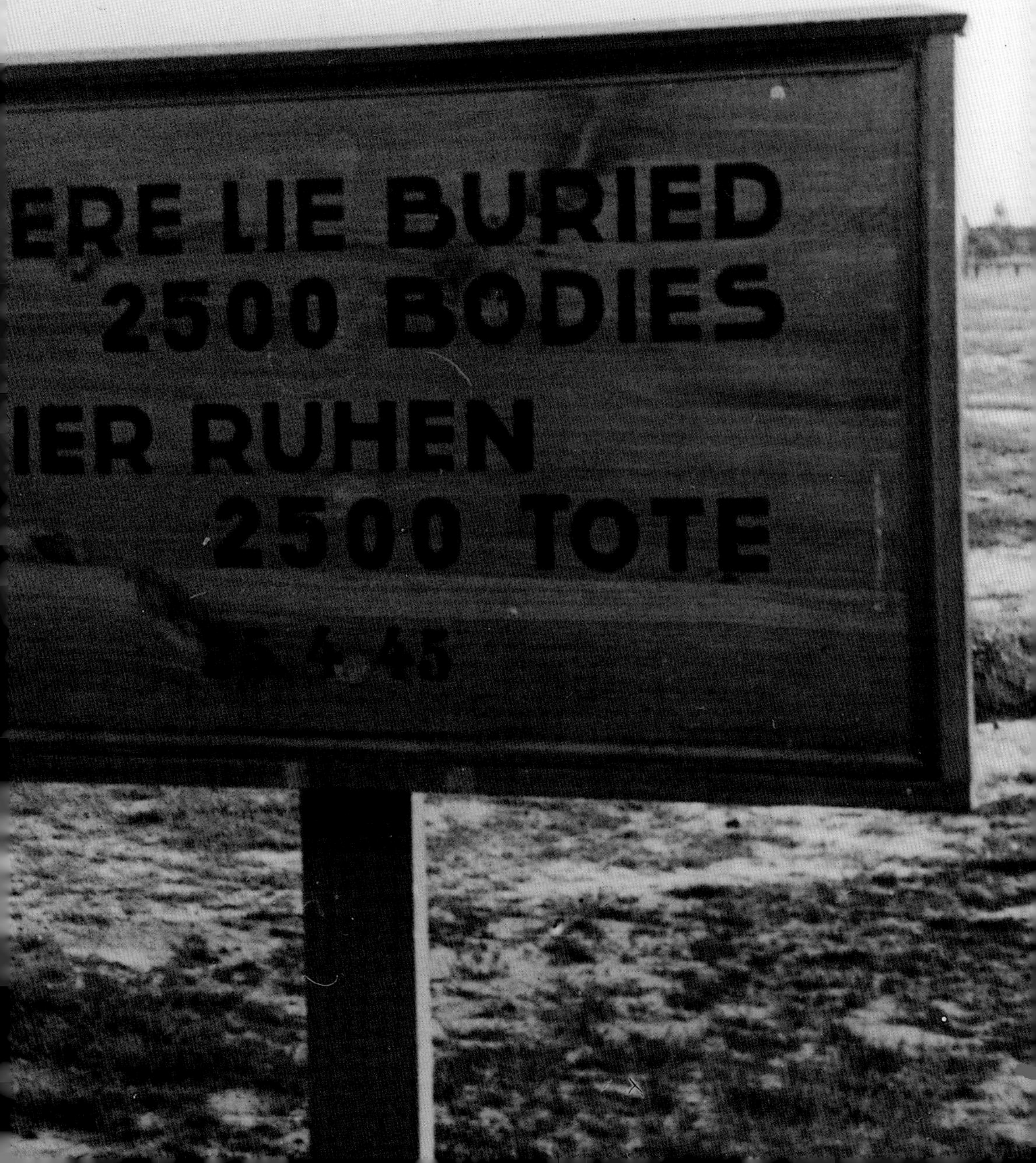
ERE LIE BURIED
2500 BODIES
IER RUHEN
2500 TOTE

Josef Rosensaft and his wife Hadassa Bimko Rosensaft attend the arrival of an Anglo-American committee of inquiry, May 15, 1947.

Josef Rosensaft (center), during the visit by an Anglo-American committee of Inquiry. May 15, 1947. Behind him is Norbert Wolheim (deputy Chairman of the Central Committee). Second from left is Carl Katz (chairman of the council of the Central Committee).

Elections for the Committee
for Bergen-Belsen, March 1947.
This committee comprised
representatives of all political
parties.

Election campaign for the
Committee for Bergen-Belsen,
March 1947.

Elections for the Committee for   1 May (labor day) demonstration
Bergen-Belsen, March 1947.   at DP camp Bergen-Belsen, 1947.

OPEN THE GATES OF PALESTI

פון די באפרייטע יידן אין דער בריטישער זאנט

2ND CONGRESS OF LIBERATED JEWS IN THE B

Jude

יזכור

Congress presidium of the
Second Congress of the Liber-
ated Jews at the opening
session, July 20, 1947. Left to
right: Berl Laufer, unknown,
Noah Barou, Norbert Wolheim,
Josef Rosensaft and Hadassa
Bimko Rosensaft.

1 May demonstration at DP camp
Bergen-Belsen, 1947.

Gathering of the Second Congress of the Liberated Jews. Left to right: Harry Goldstein, Norbert Wolheim, Josef Rosensaft, unknown and Eng. Ludwig Zeif.

1 May demonstration at DP camp Bergen-Belsen, 1947.

1 May demonstration at DP camp
Bergen-Belsen, 1947.

Exodus 47

Erik Somers and René Kok

Near the end of Zippy's album is a photo series that deals with the final leg of the dramatic journey of the legendary Exodus, the ship that came to symbolize the struggle for a Jewish state. These photographs are entirely different from the others in the album. The Exodus scenes are the work of a professional press photographer, whereas the other photographs are amateur snapshots.

At the time of the Exodus affair, massive emigration by Jewish DPs seemed a long way off. The British government was clearly uncomfortable with the tens of thousands of Jewish DPs eager to immigrate to the British Mandate area of Palestine. While the British authorities sympathized with the longing of the Jewish survivors, they accommodated Arab disapproval. Under these circumstances, the DPs began to despise the British more and more. Tensions ran so high that violent clashes with the former liberators became imminent. In the summer of 1947 the Exodus affair was about to blow up: the situation was on the verge of getting out of control.

The Exodus 47 was one of the 64 ships that transported Jewish DPs illegally between the end of the war and the proclamation of the State of Israel in May 1948. The ship – which acquired its legendary name during the voyage – weighed anchor at the harbor of Marseille with 4,554 passengers on board on July 10, 1947.[1] Seven days later, with the docks of Haifa already in sight, the British Navy boarded the ship. The passengers fought as hard as they could but were no match for the heavily armed marines. In the violence four Jewish passengers were killed and dozens injured. The illegal immigrants were transferred to three British transport vessels and taken to France. Although they were offered political asylum by the French government, most refused to go ashore. Palestine was their destination, and they would settle for nothing else. For three weeks the transport ships remained in the harbor city under disgraceful conditions. Eventually, the British sent the ships to Hamburg, where the desperate passengers were forced to debark by British military police with their rifles at the ready. They were brought to the tightly guarded Pöppendorf and Am Stau camps surrounded by barbed wire: a deeply humiliating experience for Jewish DPs who had survived the Nazi concentration camps.

Arrival in Hamburg

Zippy Orlin's album contains pictures taken by the Hamburg photographer Ursula Litzmann depicting the final stage of the Exodus saga: the arrival of the Exodus passengers from Hamburg at the train station in Lübeck, the transfer of the Jewish emigrants to the Pöppendorf and Am Stau camps, and the vehement protests that ensued at DP camp Bergen-Belsen.[2]

On September 8 the Ocean Voyager was the first of the three ships to dock at Hamburg. The next day the two others arrived: the Empire Rival and the Runnymede Park. The international press turned out en masse to document the events. But the British kept the nearly two hundred journalists well away from Pier 29 where the ships docked, behind the hastily erected barbed-wire barriers. Press representatives had to mount a special platform to watch the course of events. The actual debarkation was therefore almost entirely concealed from public view. Taking photographs was strictly prohibited. Four hundred Jews from the DP camp Bergen-Belsen came to Hamburg to show support for the Exodus passengers and to demonstrate against the British actions. They, too, were kept far away from the pier and were not able even to get a glimpse of the debarkation.[3]

Jewish organizations refused to assist the British authorities with the debarkation. The Central Committee of Liberated Jews in the British Zone asked their chairman Josef Rosensaft to communicate its refusal to become involved in the operation: "Such action would mean suspension in this zone, Jewish organizations will not be represented at the landing should it actually occur. We regard the act of the British government in bringing these people to Germany as inhuman and the worst post-war atrocity."[4]

The debarkation was heart wrenching. Many passengers heeded the instructions to leave the ship voluntarily, but with noticeable reluctance. Several refused and resisted with all their might. British troops and military police disregarded the orders to exercise restraint and used their clubs and even tear gas to drive the resisters from the ships. Men, women, and children screamed, cried, and yelled. The injured were transported to hospitals in Hamburg and Lübeck, and several DPs who continued to resist were arrested by the military police.[5]

Marguerite Higgins reported on the course of events upon the arrival of the first ship (the Ocean Voyager) in the European edition of the Herald Tribune:

Photographer Ursula Litzmann, 1948.

"Although the debarkation began peacefully, the determination of the younger male refugees not to leave the ship 'at any place but Palestine' resulted in the calling of 160 troops on board. A swirling rolling melee in the two main holds of the ship resulted between the Jews and the British military policemen. But as fists and truncheon were the only weapons used there were no serious causalities. During the debarkation the deep anger of the Jews spumed out as passenger after passenger shouted from the railing: 'The British are the new Fascists ... All we ask is a chance to live.' Several Jewish women refugees spat contemptuously as they passed the guards on deck. Below, in the shambles that reigned in the holds, this reporter saw drawings of crude Union Jacks superimposed with swastikas. This motif was repeated in the latrines."[6]

The debarkation of the second ship proceeded without a murmur. All passengers appeared to leave willingly. Later it became clear why. Upon inspecting the deserted ship, British troops found a ticking time bomb. They managed to extinguish it in time.[7]

The debarkation from the last ship (the Runnymede Park), on the other hand, was very violent. After the passengers had ignored two appeals to leave the ship voluntarily, British troops came aboard. Once again journalist Higgins was present: "The violent hand-to-hand battles followed, in which the British substituted truncheons and sprays from fire-hoses for firearms, while the Jews used anything at hand from Ukuleles, boxes and sticks around which barbed wire had been wrapped. Refugees began flinging a cascade of crates, empty tins and sticks at troops who responded by trying to grab the ringleaders. A free-for-all ensued... Even six and eight-year old children on being hoisted up the ladder to the deck would kick and bite the military policemen who formed a funnel from the holds to the gangway. About seventy-five refugees had to be carried down the gangplank and at least two out of three had to be carried at least part way on deck away from the entrance to the hold. The last corner of resistance was broken down when a fire hose was brought to play on the wall behind the resisters. The spray bounced back forming a kind of waterfall over them."[8] Altogether, 33 were injured in this final debarkation.

Pöppendorf and Am Stau

The first group of illegal immigrants traveled by train from Hamburg to Lübeck and was escorted by the British. They made the brief journey in old third-class wooden train compartments, with the doors bolted shut and windows with bars. The British had strictly prohibited photographs of the transport. The roads to the station were closed, the platform was closed off with gates and barbed wire, and signs stipulated: "Press no entry." No unauthorized individuals were allowed near the arrival of the trains. Nonetheless, Ursula Litzmann photographed their arrival at their final destination at the Lübeck-Kücknitz station. The pictures do not reveal any obstacles in the path of the German photographer. She simply
did her work from behind the barbed wire. In one picture, a British soldier looks straight into her lens.

Ursula Litzmann (born in 1916), a freelance photographer in Hamburg at the time, was assigned to photograph the event by Karl Marx, executive editor of the *Jüdische Gemeindeblatt*.[9] Karl Marx was at the site as well and interviewed passengers. At the hospital in Lübeck he spoke with those who had sustained injuries during the violent debarkation.

Litzmann is one of the few photo journalists known to have taken pictures at the station. Her photographs are the only ones preserved of the event and are therefore the only images depicting the sad end to the Exodus saga.[10] During the days that followed, her photographs were published in several international papers.[11]

The photographs reveal the exhausted Exodus passengers staggering from the trains, clutching all their worldly belongings. After a disastrous journey of sixty days, they were back "on Germany's blood-drenched soil."[12] Screened from public view, the DPs walk down the platforms past a cordon of British soldiers and board the trucks waiting to take them to the Pöppendorf and Am Stau refugee camps. The faces of the returnees reflect indignation and disbelief. Some British soldiers are visibly moved. Overall, the refugees appear stoic and bear traces of the recent skirmishes at the debarkation in Hamburg. One of the photographs of the platform in Lübeck depicts a woman carrying a small child and dragging her luggage in her other hand, while a British soldier watches with his hands behind his back. Many refused any assistance whatsoever from the despised British. Another photograph reveals an unconscious old woman who has been lifted from the train and placed on a stretcher. A British MP drags a somewhat older child, who is either unwilling or unable to walk.

The Jewish immigrants were taken in trucks to Camp Pöppendorf, which was less than a kilometer away, and to Camp Am Stau, which was two kilometers away. On every vehicle there were two British troops armed with sten guns. The infirm, pregnant women, and the elderly were taken by ambulance.

Litzmann also photographed the arrival of the trucks at Camp Pöppendorf. She managed to take photographs inside the camp as well. The sight of Camp Pöppendorf must have filled the Jewish DPs with horror and disbelief. Everything about the site was reminiscent of the concentration camps of the Nazi era. Pöppendorf was surrounded by barbed wire, and heavily armed British soldiers stood guard in the watchtowers. The pictures in Zippy Orlin's album reveal the trucks entering the camp site and the gate with its bars closing behind the illegal immigrants. Zippy's caption to these pictures reads: "Clutching their meagre possessions the 4,500 enter the hell that Amstau and Pöppendorf proved to be" (p. 101). The inmates were registered at the camp. The procedure was extremely disorganized, since many refused to cooperate in principle and would not disclose their names or personal data. They were unwilling to identify themselves for fear that the Exodus group might be split up and each member returned to the DP camp they'd come from. The British authorities recorded names such as Charlie Chaplin and Greta Garbo or compound identities such as Adolf Bevin.[13] The International Refugee Organization of the United Nations promised that the stranded travelers would retain their status as Displaced Persons, but this offer was rejected by the DPs. "We are not DPs, we are in transit to Palestine," recorded a British official.[14] The Exodus passengers were deloused and underwent a brief medical inspection. Afterwards, they each received three sheets and a bowl of hot soup.

Reactions at Bergen-Belsen

The Exodus problem occasioned severe indignation at DP camp Bergen-Belsen, especially since many Belsen DPs were among the Exodus passengers. The affair was the last straw in the worsening relations with the British. In the early hours of September 7, 1947, the day before the first ship with the returning illegal immigrants arrived in Hamburg, virtually the entire camp population staged an unplanned demonstration. Bringing Jewish emigrants back to Germany, where all had personally experienced the horrors of the Holocaust, was regarded as intolerable and consequently as a declaration of war by the British against the Jews. The crowd that had gathered chanted anti-British epithets, and tensions ran high.

The leadership of the Jewish community in the British Zone did all it could to quell the anger, fearing that a revolt was a distinct possibility.[15] Jewish leaders believed that violence on the part of the Jewish DPs could jeopardize a carefully

Aboard the Runnymede Park, passengers of the Exodus 1947 put up a self-made flag. Barbed wire and an iron enclosure converted the hospital ship into a transport ship for prisoners.

Debarkation of illegal emigrants
from deportation ship
Runnymede Park, Hamburg,
September 9, 1947.

devised diplomatic solution to the immigration problem, as well as the establishment of the State of Israel. In the afternoon a more formal protest gathering was
hastily convened.[16] The photographer Ursula Litzmann attended. Zippy's album
contains nine photographs of the events that occurred at the camp that day.
Five thousand DPs met on Freedom Square. They chanted anti-British epithets,
carried banners, and waved flags featuring Jewish and Zionist symbols.
Josef Rosensaft, chairman of the Central Committee of the Liberated Jews in
the British Zone, was one of the speakers. He vehemently condemned the
British actions and promised full support for the passengers from the Exodus.
At the same time, he urged his audience to avoid a violent confrontation with
the British.[17] Other speakers that afternoon included Dr. Noah Barou of the
World Jewish Congress from London and Marc Jarblum of the Jewish Agency
for Palestine from Paris. In their speeches, they also tried to calm the fervor
among those present and urged them not to respond to the "British terror"
in kind.[18] The gathering was fairly orderly. The success of the Jewish leaders
in containing the anger and dissatisfaction averted unrest. The only minor incident that occurred was when a dummy representing the controversial British
Foreign Secretary Ernest Bevin was set on fire and trampled by bystanders.
According to the official AJDC report, several Jewish youths, who had been
incited by journalists and press photographers eager to capture sensational
scenes, were responsible for this incident.[19] Zippy's album includes a Litzmann
photograph of the event.

Surrounded by barbed wire

The Pöppendorf and Am Stau camps where the Exodus immigrants were
brought had been prepared very hastily just before their arrival. Pöppendorf,
the larger of the two, was situated between Lübeck and the village of Traven-
münde. Since the summer of 1945, the site had served as a POW camp for
German troops. That November it started to be used as a camp for non-Jewish
refugees from East Germany. The smaller camp at Am Stau had housed Polish
Displaced Persons.

In the days before the Exodus travelers arrived, hundreds of Yugoslav DPs
had been deployed under British supervision to prepare the camp grounds.
The East European refugees who had been staying in these camps were quickly
transferred. Gates with bars over two meters high and four meters wide and
lined with rolls of barbed wire were placed around the camp, and watchtowers
with floodlights were built. Families were assigned to the 125 tents intended to
accommodate six people. Groups who wanted to stay together were housed
in Nissan huts with iron roofs (Wellblechbaracken).

The British authorities requested the German civilian staff in charge of the
records of the East European refugees and camp management to stay on.
They were screened, however, and were required to complete questionnaires.

The main concern of the British was to protect the DPs from encounters with former Nazis. The German camp commander instructed his staff as follows: "In the carrying out of their duty to show the greatest restraint in respect of the Jews, and on no condition to get involved in an exchange of words or dispute."[20]

The Exodus immigrants staged a protest the very first day, with slogans comparing the British Secretary Bevin to Hitler. The German camp staff were the main targets of their discontent. "Down with the German camp administration," they chanted. That morning they distributed 4,500 leaflets throughout the camp, in which the Jewish community and the Haganah (the secret organization that arranged illegal immigration to Palestine) expressed their solidarity with the Exodus passengers. The leaflets were printed at the DP camp Bergen-Belsen and smuggled onto the site.[21]

The protests in the camp continued. Chaired by Mordechai Rosmann, a Jewish committee was organized to deal with the British authorities and the German camp staff. The Jewish camp population continued to refuse to register. In addition to their fierce opposition to disclosing information to German officials, they feared that agreeing to register could lead to reprisals for their efforts to immigrate illegally: it was possible they might be excluded from any official exit permits.

Jewish relief organizations were allowed to enter the camps, and the relief effort got under way five days after the refugees arrived. The American Jewish Joint Distribution Committee supplied clothing and cigarettes and provided kosher meals. A kosher kitchen opened shortly thereafter. Food packages arrived from all over the world – especially from the United States and Canada – as a token of sympathy for the stranded immigrants. Inhabitants from Lübeck and the surrounding area donated vegetables, fruit, and other food to the Jewish community, and the DPs at Belsen took up a collection as well.

After two weeks the Jewish Relief Unit staff assumed responsibility for medical care and hygiene. Jewish doctors and nurses replaced the German care providers. The exhausted camp inmates soon regained their health. Hygiene, however, remained a concern: there was not enough drinking water, and the restroom facilities were inadequate.

Social and cultural activities gradually got under way at both camps. Mornings started with exercises and raising the flag with the star of David. Over eight hundred children received instruction from Jewish teachers, and a kindergarten opened for the very youngest. Adults attended English lessons. Movies were shown, and music and dance performances were organized. Religion was important as well. Temporary synagogues were set up for morning prayer services. Rabbis made frequent visits to the camp to organize joint prayers and to offer support as needed.

The general impression was that the British authorities aimed to punish the illegal immigrants for their acts with poor accommodations and a heavy-handed approach.[22] But the British harsh treatment had a different basis: they did not know what to do with the Exodus passengers. They hoped that the illegal immigrants would agree to be transferred to France or to accept official refugee status from the International Refugee Organization in return for improved living conditions. The inmates, however, refused to consider these options. The *ma'apalim* (illegal immigrants) regarded themselves as citizens of Palestine who had been deported illegally by the British and were entitled to return.[23] In the end, the British had no choice but to accept the presence of the Exodus passengers in their sector. The camp regimen was relaxed, due in part to international pressure.

The tents, Nissan huts, and other facilities were sorely inadequate for the cold winter months. The British authorities therefore decided to transfer the camp inmates to better accommodations in Emden and Sengwarden, north of Wilhelmshaven in East Friesland. Representatives of the Jewish camp committee and the AJDC visited the sites. They liked the new accommodations and approved the move.[24] As a sign of the good relations with the German camp staff at that point, the individuals concerned requested that the German staff be transferred with them. Unfortunately, this was not feasible.[25]

Between November 2 and 5, 1947, the British transferred the inmates from Camp Pöppendorf to their new accommodations. A few days later the ones from Camp Am Stau followed. Most did not stay long. Many were soon permitted to leave for Palestine via the American Zone of Occupation. Several camp inmates snucked out of the camp and into Camp Bergen-Belsen, where they obtained assistance to enter Palestine illegally. By March 1948, about 1,000 Exodus passengers had reached their final destination of Palestine. One month later 1,800 of the original 4,500 Exodus passengers remained in the two refugee camps in East Friesland. By the summer of 1948, the Central Committee arranged for the few Exodus passengers still there to be transferred to Bergen-Belsen, pending their emigration.[26] That August a large group of over 500 former Exodus passengers was authorized to board the train for Marseille, where they were finally able to make their long-awaited journey to the new State of Israel.

The Exodus affair

Escorted by British troops, the Exodus passengers arrive at Lübeck-Kücknitz Station, September 9, 1947.

Escorted by British troops, the
passengers of the Exodus arrive
at the Lübeck-Kücknitz Station.
September 9, 1947.

An injured woman receives first aid. Lübeck-Kücknitz Station, September 9, 1947

Lübeck-Kücknitz Station.

Passengers of the Exodus are taken in trucks to the Am Stau and Pöppendorf refugee camps. Lübeck-Kücknitz Station.

Five thousand indignant DPs at Bergen-Belsen demonstrate against the British decision to force the passengers of the Exodus to return to Germany. Dr. Noah Barou, a leader of the World Jewish Congress in London, addresses a rally. Behind him is Josef Rosensaft. September 7, 1947.

Demonstration against the
actions of the British in the
Exodus affair, September 7, 1947.

A young man tramples a charred
effigy of Ernest Bevin, the British
Minister of Foreign Affairs.
September 7, 1947.

British troops escort the Exodus
passengers into the tightly
guarded Pöppendorf refugee
camp. September 9, 1947.

Exodus passengers await
medical examinations at camp
Pöppendorf.

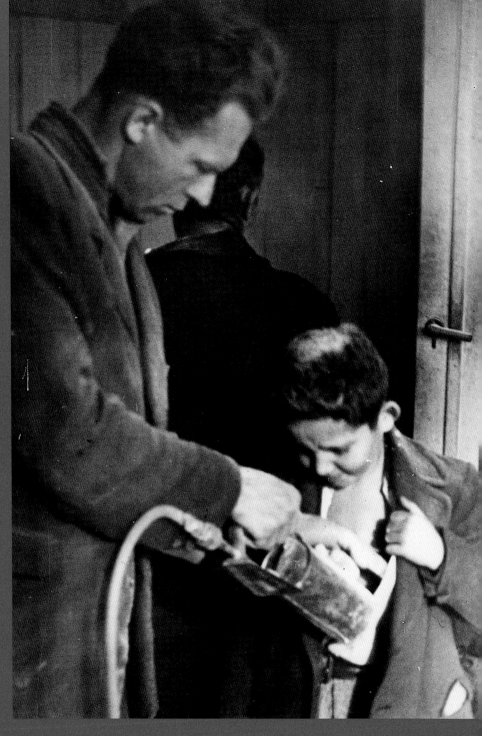

Arranging the bedrooms,
Pöppendorf, September 9, 1947.

Delousing.

Processing administrative data
and distributing soup.

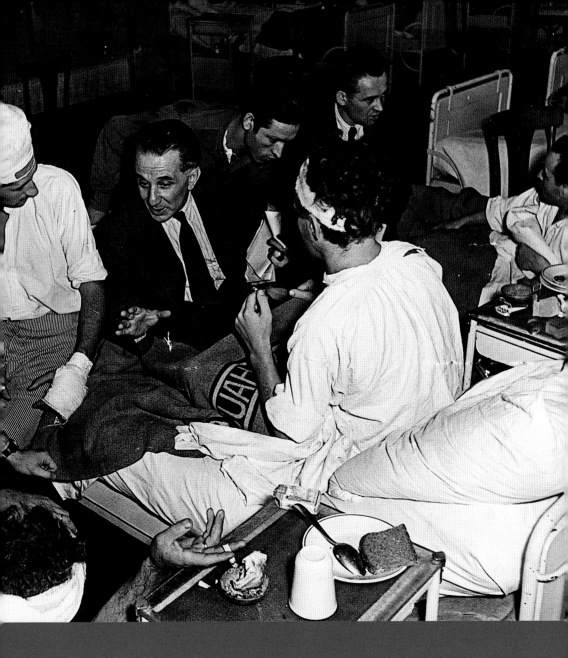

Discussion among the Exodus
passengers, Pöppendorf,
September 9, 1947.

Distributing soup.

At the hospital in Lübeck,
Karl Marx, executive editor of
the *Jüdische Gemeindeblatt*,
interviews illegal emigrants
injured during the debarkation
in Hamburg. September 9, 1947.

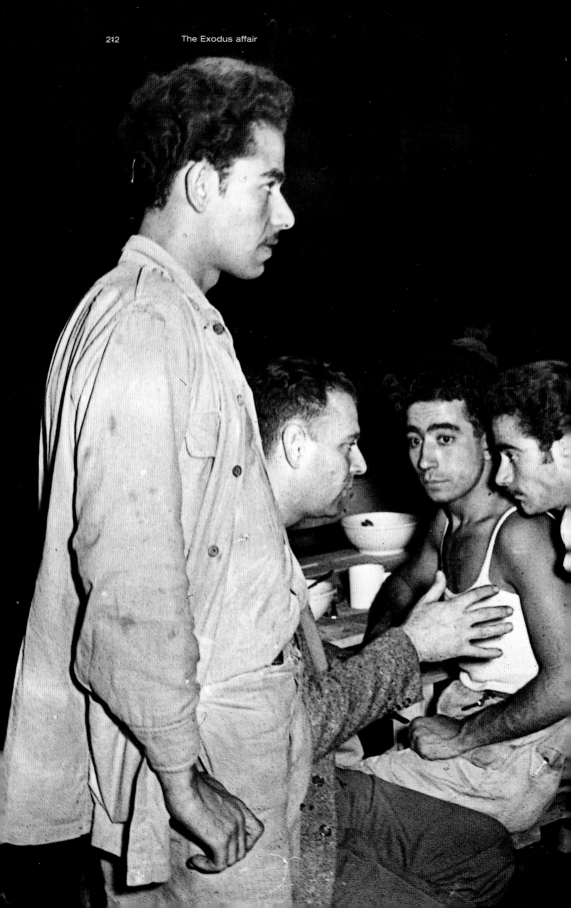

Emotional passengers of the Exodus at Pöppendorf refugee camp, September 9, 1947.

Eyewitnesses

Genya Markon

Reuma Schwartz Weizman

Born in London, Reuma Schwartz Weizman immigrated to Palestine with her parents when she was just a year old. In 1945, after completing her studies, she returned to London to improve her English. During her first summer there, the Jewish Agency arranged for her to work with children who had been rescued from the Holocaust and were being adopted by the Jewish community in London. At summer's end she was sent by the Jewish Agency to cover the Nuremberg trials, along with other journalists. She remained there for two weeks, reporting for a Jewish news outlet in London. At that time, "Not all the horrors and agonies of the Holocaust were known to us," she writes. She also states that she described her experiences in letters to her father, some of which were published in the Palestine Post. What she learned at Nuremberg inspired her to seek further work with survivors, convinced that she had to contribute to their rehabilitation. Reuma was assigned a job at Blankenese, and she appears in a staff photo in the Orlin album.

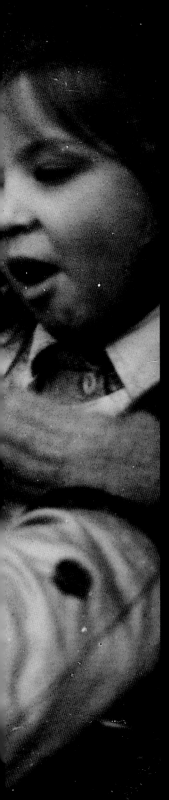

John Fink

John Fink, originally named Hans Finke, was born in Berlin in 1920. He was raised by his merchant father Julius, and his stepmother Ella. As Nazi restrictions increased, Hans' father thought it prudent that his son learn a trade. Hans was duly apprenticed to an electrician and passed the difficult journeyman's exams. The Finke family remained in Berlin, and Hans remembers carrying the required Kennkarte (I.D. card) with a red "J" stamped on it. In March 1943 he was arrested and deported to Auschwitz, where he was put to work in the I. G. Farben Buna factory in Monowitz. During his two years there, and subsequently in the concentration camps of Sachsenhausen, Flossenburg, and finally at the "convalescent camp" of Bergen-Belsen, his training as an electrician helped him survive. Upon his liberation on April 15, 1945, he weighed only 80 pounds. Nevertheless, he was able to help the British engineers restore power to the camp, and he witnessed the burning of the Bergen-Belsen barracks to curb the spread of typhus. After rehabilitation he went to work for the Joint in the Blankenese children's home. A year later he married Alice Redlich, a German-born nurse serving with a British war relief organization.

John Fink escorts children about to depart for Palestine, 1947.

Sally Wideroff

Sally Wideroff, a trained social worker from New York City, was sent by the Joint to help rehabilitate child survivors in the Bergen-Belsen DP camp. Later she helped set up the Blankenese children's home near Hamburg, some fifty miles from Belsen in Germany's British Zone. After five decades she still recalls how she selected pastel-colored wall paints to brighten the children's lives, how she put pictures and potted plants in their rooms to welcome them. Unimportant details in ordinary circumstances, but these were hardly ordinary circumstances. Most of these youngsters were orphans who had been deprived of their childhood. Giving it back was no easy task, and political circumstances intervened in the children's rehabilitation.

Each month, the British distributed a number of immigration certificates for Palestine to orphan children who resided in their zone, and the Jewish Agency decided to smuggle children from other parts of Europe into the zone by setting up an official residence for them there.

The orphanage was located in the former estate of the prominent German-Jewish family, the Warburgs. Confiscated by the Nazis during the war, the estate was donated to the Joint in 1946 by the Warburgs to serve as a children's home. In fact, it became a way station for children en route to Palestine, and many of them spent only a few weeks at Blankenese. From there, Sally Wideroff and others escorted them on trains to Marseilles, where the JDC had ships awaiting them.

"At each station," Sally remembers, "Limoges, Lyon, the children danced on the platform while we phoned the Jewish Welfare Board or the Red Cross to meet us at the next station with matzot and cocoa. When we arrived, some American soldiers came down from the hills and we had an outdoor Passover that cannot be forgotten."

In a postscript she adds, "I still hear the children's voices coming from the ship Champollion, singing "Oh! What a Beautiful Morning" from the Broadway play "Oklahoma" as they faded away across the blue-green Mediterranean to their welcome in Palestine/Israel."

Sally (wearing gloves) amid
schoolchildren and teachers.
December 1946.

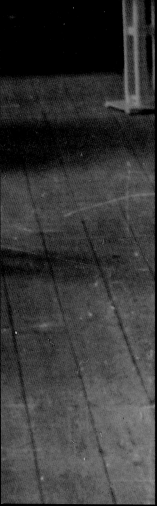

and Maria Amborski. Childless themselves, the Amborskis eventually became her rescuers, agreeing to hide her for the duration of the war. They also took in her mother Dora, who posed as Josef's sister, but as the danger of being discovered grew, Dora had to leave. After the war, Dora and Stefa were reunited and sent to the displaced persons camp of Bergen-Belsen, where they remained until their immigration to the USA in 1950.

Steffa, far right, with the doll she carried all those years beside her.

Nandor Aron

Nandor Aron was born on June 26, 1926 in Cluj, Romania. During the war
Cluj became the capital of Hungarian-ruled northern Transylvania, which
was affected by the war only late in the spring of 1944. In the first week of
May, however, 18,000 Jews were forced into a ghetto established in the
local brickyard. Nandor lived in the ghetto for a month before being transported to Auschwitz, whence he was transferred to work in a munitions
factory, building cannons for the German army in a sub-camp of Gross
Rosen in Lower Silesia. When Soviet troops liberated Nandor in May 1945,
at the age of nineteen, he returned to his home town of Cluj and spent
some months working for the Joint until he heard that his sister was alive
in Bergen-Belsen. He set out to find her there, only to discover that she
had been sent to Sweden for treatment of tuberculosis, where she died.
Soon after his arrival at Belsen, Nandor met Anna Rosenbluth from
Hungary; they wed on May 19, 1946. For the next three years Nandor
served as a policeman in the camp and played an active role in the *Hagibor Hachshara* (Zionist collective), consisting largely of survivors from
Cluj.

Jewish policeman Nandor Aron
on guard during the dedication of
the Bergen-Belsen memorial,
April 15, 1946.

Hilde Goldberg Jacobstahl

Hilde Jacobstahl, the daughter of Walter and Betty Jacobstahl, was born in Berlin in 1925. Her father designed and manufactured women's clothing. In 1929 the family moved to Amsterdam, where her father became active in the Jewish religious Reform Movement. Together with Otto Frank, Anne Frank's father, Walter founded the Reform Congregation in Amsterdam. He also began helping the other refugees who sought a safe haven in The Netherlands from the increasing persecution in Austria and Germany. Despite the deteriorating situation, the Jacobstahls made no attempt to leave the Netherlands. Hilde was able to continue her high school education until the Jews were barred from public schools, and she trained to be an early childhood teacher. After the Amsterdam ghetto was established, she worked with the childcare center in front of the Hollandsche Schouwburg, the place where children were sent to hiding places, with the collaboration of the Dutch underground.

On her return from a brief stay in the countryside in July 1943, Hilde discovered that her parents had been deported. She made her way to Belgium to join her elder brother Joachim, who was fighting in the resistance. Joachim was eventually captured and interned in a camp for resistance fighters, where he was sentenced to death. A week before his scheduled execution he was liberated by the British. Hilde, too, worked for the underground. Following Belgium's liberation by the British, she went to Brussels, where she was attached to the British Red Cross. Her first tour of duty was in the DP camp of Belsen, arriving with the first British military and medical units on April 15. In addition to nursing the survivors, Hilde served as their translator, speaking four languages. Her next assignment was at Blankenese, where she taught kindergarten. During her stay in Belsen, Hilde met and married Max Goldberg, a doctor who worked as an UNRAA Public health Officer and who had come from Switzerland to help the survivors.

Hilde Jacobstahl and Dr. Fritz Spanier, director of the Belsen hospital.

Notes

Introduction

1   *Oorlogsdocumentatie.
Negende jaarboek van het Rijksin-
stituut voor Oorlogsdocumentatie*,
eds G. Aalders, N.D.J. Barnouw,
M. Berman, D. van Galen Last,
G. Hirschfeld, M. de Keizer, R. Kok,
P. Romijn, E. Somers, H. de Vries,
Zutphen, 1998, pp. 145-146.

2   *www.niod.nl.*

3   Eric Nooter, "Displaced
Persons from Bergen-Belsen,
the JDC photographic Archives"
in *History of Photography*, Volume
23, No. 4, Winter 1999, guest
editors Sybil Milton & Genya
Markon, pp. 331-339. Eric Nooter
article.

4   Menachem Z. Rosensaft (Ed.).
Life reborn. Jewish Displaced
Persons 1945-1951, Conference
Proceedings, Washington, D.C.,
January 14-17, 2000. A project
of the United States Holocaust
Memorial Museum and Its Second
Generation Advisory Group in
association with the American
Jewish Joint Distribution Commit-
tee.

5   Quotation from Rachel van
Amerongen-Frankfoorder in Willy
Lindwer, "De laatste zeven Maan-
den, Vrouwen in het voetspoor van
Anne Frank," Hilversum, 1988.

6   Hagit Lavsky, *New Beginnings.
Holocaust Survivors in Bergen-
Belsen and the British Zone in Ger-
many, 1945-1950*, Detroit, 2002.

7   Throughout the 1990s, for
example, the NIOD made large
microfilm sections of its own
archives and photo collection
regarding the persecution of the
Jews available to the USHMM. This
cooperation recently culminated in
the exhibition *Anne Frank the
Writer; an Unfinished Story*, which
was featured in the second part of
2003 in honor of the tenth anniversary of the USHMM. The NIOD
provided Anne Frank's original
diaries and other writings on standing loan from its collection on this
occasion. This was the first time
these writings by Anne Frank were
exhibited outside the Anne Frank
House in Amsterdam.

The Album and Zippy Orlin

1   Most of the information about
Zippy Orlin comes from interviews
that Erik Somers and René Kok
conducted with Bluma Rubin-Orlin
(Antwerp, August 29 and September 8, 1997) and Harry "Zvi" Orlin
(Tel Aviv, October 28, 1997) and
from Genya Markon's interviews
with Harry Orlin (… March 2003)
and Nanou Huybrechts (Amsterdam, August 29, 1997).

2   *S.A. Reconstruction*, June 1,
1946, p. 7.

3   Joanne Reilly, *Belsen. The
Liberation of a Concentration
Camp* (London/New York, 1998),
pp. 87-88.

4   Noah Barou, "Remembering
Belsen" in *Belsen, Irgun Sheerit
hapleita Me'Haezor Habriti*
(publ./ed. Tel Aviv/London, 1957),
p. 83, and Hagit Lavsky, *New
Beginnings, Holocaust Survivors
in Bergen-Belsen and the British
Zone in Germany, 1945-1950*,
Detroit, 2002, pp. 142-143. Angelika Königseder and Juliane Wetzel,
*Lebensmut im Wartesaal, Die jüdis-
chen DPs (Displaced Persons) im
Nachkriegsdeutschland.* (Frankfurt
am Main, 1995), pp. 139-146.

5   Angelika Königseder and
Juliane Wetzel, *Lebensmut im
Wartesaal*, pp. 66-69.

6   *Ibid.*, p. 47 and p. 265. See also
the article by Thomas Rahe elsewhere in this publication.

7   JDC report, Central Committee, 31-35 in Hagit Lavsky, *New
Beginnings*, p. 150 and p. 167.

8   Hagit Lavsky, "A Community of
Survivors: Bergen-Belsen as a
Jewish Center after 1945" in:
Joanne Reilly, David Cesarani, Tony
Kushner and Colin Richmond (eds),
Belsen in History and Memory
(London 1970), p. 170.

9   Letter from "The Belsen Trans-
port in Merano" to S[Z]ippy,
Merano, 8 May 1947. NIOD, Doc I,
Cecilia "Zippy" Orlin.

10   Josef Rosensaft, "Our Belsen,"
in *Belsen, Irgun Sheerit Hapleita
Me'Haezor Habriti* (publ./ed.)
(Tel Aviv 1957), pp. 39-40.

11   C. Orlin, "What it's really like in a D.P. Camp" in *The Zionist Record*, 4 March 1949. See elsewhere in this book. Captions to photographs from the album of Zippy Orlin.

12   Angelika Königseder and Juliane Wetzel, *Lebensmut im Wartesaal*, p. 265.

13   Hagit Lavsky, *New Beginnings*, pp. 210-211.

14   Service rating form AJDC rated by Samuel Dallob, drafted on 6 September 1948 and signed on 28 September 1948. NIOD, Doc I, Cecillia "Zippy" Orlin.

15   C. Orlin, "What it's really like in a D.P. Camp" in *The Zionist Record*, 4 March 1949. See elsewhere in this book.

16   Zippy Orlin's photo album, p. 73.

17   Interview conducted by Genya Markon with Harry "Zvi" Orlin (Tel Aviv, January 2003).

DP Camp 1945-1950: The British Section

1. For extensive details about the general context of the Jewish DP history, see: Angelika Königseder / Juliane Wetzel, *Lebensmut im Wartesaal. Die jüdischen DPs (Displaced Persons) im Nachkriegsdeutschland*, Frankfurt a. M., 1994. English translation: *Waiting for Hope. Jewish Displaced Persons in Post-World War II Germany*, Evanston, 2001. On Belsen and the British Zone, see the excellent work by Joanne Reilly, *Belsen. The Liberation of a Concentration Camp*, London / New York, 1998. Only a few new insights appear in the work by Hagit Lavsky, New *Beginnings. Holocaust Survivors in Bergen-Belsen and the British Zone in Germany, 1945-1950*, Detroit, 2002.

2   Reilly, *Belsen*, p. 17.

3   Quoted from Eberhard Kolb, *Bergen-Belsen, 1943-1945*, Göttingen, 1985, p. 49. (Translation: Königseder / Wetzel, *Waiting for Hope*, p. 168.)

4   Reilly, *Belsen*, p. 18.

5   Rainer Schulze, "Die Briten und das DP-Camp Bergen-Belsen, 1945-1950," lecture delivered at the specialist convention on the redesign of the Bergen-Belsen memorial, November 4-6, 2002.

6   Quoted from Yehuda Bauer, Flight and Rescue: Brichah, New York, 1970, p. 7.

7   The late arrival of the relief organizations is primarily attributa-

ble to the restrictive disposition of the responsible military authorities, who aimed to prevent civilian interference.

8   Quoted from Leonard Dinnerstein, *America and the Survivors of the Holocaust*, New York, 1982, p. 292.

9   Ibid.

10   YIVO Institute for Jewish Research, New York (YIVO), files Leo W. Schwarz Papers fol. 52. H. Viteles, Report on Visit to Germany, January 6-April 8, 1946, p. 54. (Microfilm edition, see also: Zentrum für Antisemitismusforschung, Technische Universität Berlin).

11   Quoted from Reilly, *Belsen*, p. 108.

12   Sigrun Jochims, "Lübeck ist nur eine kurze Station auf dem jüdischen Wanderweg", *Jüdisches Leben in Schleswig-Holstein 1945-1950*, Thesis, TU Berlin, Berlin, 2003, p. 20.

13   Dinnerstein, *America and the Survivors*, p. 295.

14   Samuel Gringauz, "Jewish Destiny as the DPs See It. The Ideology of the Surviving Remnant," in *Commentary* vol. 4 (December 1947), p. 503.

15   Yehuda Bauer, *Out of the Ashes. The Impact of American Jews on Post-Holocaust European Jewry*, Oxford, 1989, p. 48.

16   The matter is discussed extensively in Thomas Albrich, *Exodus durch Österreich. Die jüdischen Flüchtlinge 1945-1948*, Innsbruck, 1987, p. 31.

17   Ibid., p. 80.

18   Quoted from Schulze, lecture delivered in November 2002.

19   Albrich, *Exodus durch Österreich*, p. 80; Reilly, *Belsen*, p. 100.

20   Quoted from Schulze lecture.

21   Quoted from Jochims, Lübeck, p. 37.

22   Quoted from Jochims, Lübeck, p. 38.

23   Dinnerstein, *America and the Survivors*, pp. 111.

24   Reilly, *Belsen*, p. 104.

25   Quoted from Ibid., p. 105.

26   Ibid., p. 110.

27   *Jüdisches Gemeindeblatt*, Düsseldorf, March 25, 1949.

Social Life in the Jewish DP Camp at Bergen-Belsen

1   On the subsequent course of events, cf. Angelika Königseder /

Juliane Wezel, *Lebensmut im Wartesaal. Die Jüdischen DP's (Displaced Persons) im Nachkriegsdeutschland*, Frankfurt/M., 1994, pp. 173-218; Hagit Lavsky, *A Community of Survivors: Bergen-Belsen as a Jewish Centre after 1945*, in Jo Reilly *et al.* (ed.), *Belsen in History and Memory*, London/Portland, 1997, pp. 162-177; Hagit Lavsky, *New Beginnings. Holocaust Survivors in Bergen-Belsen and the British Zone in Germany, 1945-1950*, Detroit, 2002.

2   Report from Shlomo Michael Gelber, American Jewish Joint Distribution Committee in the following: JDC, June 28, 1946 (JDC Archives, New York: File 395 Germany, Displaced Persons Camp, Bergen-Belsen, 1945).

3   A. Königseder / J. Wetzel (see Note 1), p. 265.

4   Report from R. G. Morren UNRRA Director, Team 806, February 10, 1947 (United Nations Archives, New York: PAG-4/3.0.11.2.0.2.B. 117).

5   "There are no Jews over the age of 40 or 45 years in Belsen," read a rather terse report from Maurice Eigen (JDC) August 31, 1945 (JDC Archives, New York: File 395 Germany, Displaced Persons Camp, Bergen-Belsen, 1945).

6   Report from R. G. Morren (see note 4); report from M. Eigen (see note 5).

7   Central Committee account, issued as the Central Committee of liberated Jews in the British Zone 1945-1947 (Bergen-Belsen 1947), p. 25. The total figure of 1,438 marriages includes 362 performed before the liberation and confirmed at the Bergen-Belsen DP camp.

8   Report from Mordecai Rosman (JDC) November 9, 1947 (JDC Archives, New York: File 388 Germany, Displaced Persons Camps, 7/1947-12/1947); report from Bertha Weingreen (Jewish Relief Unit) of April 24, 1946 (Wiener Library, London: Henriques Archive 6 B/1-23).

9   Central Committee of Liberated Jews in the British Zone (see note 7), p. 70 ff.

10   Report on a Visit by Judge Rifkind to Hohne Camp on December 20, 1945 (Archives Nationales, Paris: AJ /43/59); Rev. A. Greenbaum, *Report on Belsen* (Wiener Library, London: Henriques Archive 6 B/1-23).

11   Report from Mordecai Rosman (see note 8). On this subject, see also H. Nerson, "Rapport sur la situation au camp de Bergen-Belsen," in: Union O.S.E. (ed.), "Rapports sur la situation des Juifs en Allemagne Octobre/Décembre 1945," Geneva 1945, p. 56 ff.
12   H. Nerson, Rapport sur la situation au camp de Bergen-Belsen, p. 52.
13   Joseph Wolhandler, "On a Concentration Camp Stage. Bergen-Belsen Players Depict Horrors of Their Internment," in New York Times (June 30, 1946). On the history of the Kazet-Theater, see also Nicholas Yantian, "Aus der Versteinerung heraustreten" – Das "Kazet-Theater" im jüdischen "Displaced Persons"-Lager Bergen-Belsen, 1945-1947," in Herbert Obenhaus (ed.), Im Schatten des Holocaust. Jüdisches Leben in Niedersachsen nach 1945, Hannover, 1997, pp. 131-147; Samy Feder, "The Yiddish Theatre of Belsen," in Belsen. Published by Irgun Sheerit Hapleita Me'Haezor Habriti, Tel Aviv, 1957, pp. 135-139.
14   Our Destruction in Pictures. Collected and edited by Rafael Olevski, Dawid Rosental, Paul Trepman, Bergen-Belsen 1946. The three editors were also in charge of Undzer Sztyme.
15   B. Kosowski, Bibliographie der jüdischen Ausgaben in der Britischen Zone Deutschlands 1945-1950, Bergen-Belsen, 1950.
16   Anita Lasker-Wallfisch, Ihr sollt die Wahrheit erben. Die Cellistin von Auschwitz. Erinnerungen, Reinbek, 2000, p. 189 ff.
17   Report from R. G. Morren (see Note 4).
18   Report from M. Eigen (see note 5); interview by Hagit Lavsky with Isaac Levy of March 6, 1991 (Hebrew University of Jerusalem, Institute of Contemporary Jewry: Oral History Division (1956) 2); interview by Hagit Lavsky with Norbert Wollheim of July 12, 1990 (Hebrew University of Jerusalem, Institute of Contemporary Jewry: Oral History Division (1956) 1); document by Rev. A. Greenbaum (618, Mil. Gov. Det.) of November 13, 1945 (Wiener Library, London: Henriques Archive 6 B/1-23).
19   Central Committee of liberated Jews in the British Zone (see Note 7), p. 71.
20   A. Königseder/ J. Wetzel (see note 1), p. 212. In February 1947 the UNRRA reached a similar assessment: only 15 to 30 percent of the Jewish DPs wanted to emigrate to a country other than Palestine. Report from R. G. Morren (see note 4).

The American Jewish Joint Distribution Committee and Bergen-Belsen

1   Texts from Eric Nooter's work included in this article have been taken from Eric Nooter, "Displaced Persons from Bergen-Belsen: The JDC Photographic Archives," History of Photography, Volume 23, Number 4 (Winter 1999), pp. 331-440.
2   Yehuda Bauer, Out of the Ashes: The Impact of American Jews on Post Holocaust European Jewry, New York and Oxford, 1989, xiii.
3   For early JDC history see Yehuda Bauer, My Brother's Keeper. A History of the American Jewish Joint Distribution Committee 1929-1939, Philadelphia, 1974, and American Jewry and the Holocaust: The American Jewish Joint Distribution Committee 1939-1945, Detroit, 1981.
4   The Brichah was the semi-legal flight of Jews from postwar Poland to the British and American Zones of Germany on their way to Palestine.
5   Aliyah Bet was the illegal immigration of Holocaust survivors to Palestine.
6   For the DP camp period see Bauer, Out of the Ashes; "Der joint: Amerikanisch-judische Lebenshilfe aus Ubersee" [The Joint: American Jewish Aid from Overseas], in Angelika Konigseder and Juliane Wetzel, Lebensmut im Wartesaal. Die judischen DPs (Displaced Persons) im Nachtkriegsdeutschland [The Courage to Live in the Waiting Room. The Jewish DPs in Postwar Germany], Frankfurt, 1994, 58-80.
7   JDC NY Archives, AR45/64, file 395. For moving eyewitness accounts by inmates from The Netherlands see two unpublished reports by Gertrude van Tijn: "Camp 'BergenBelsen'," in "Contribution towards the History of the Jews in Holland from May 10, 1940 to June 1944", Jerusalem, 92-115, which includes an English translation of a report by Helmuth Mainz,

the JDC Archives AR, 33/44: No. 697: Countries. Holland. Reports and 'Bergen-Belsen' in "Memoirs" Portland 1969, 82-105. Idem No. 698: Documents by Gertrude van Tijn; Abel J. Herzberg, Tweestromenland. Dagboek uit Bergen-Belsen, Arnhem, 1950, which was published in an English language edition as Between Two Streams. Diary from Bergen-Belsen, London/New York, 1997, Loden Vogel, Dagboek uit een kamp [Diary from a Camp], Amsterdam, 1965, and Jona Oberski, Kinderjaren, published in an English translation as Childhood, New York, 1984; see also J. Presser, "Bergen-Belsen", in Ondergang. De Vervolging en Verdeling van het Nederlandse Jodendom 1940-1945, Den Haag, 1965, vol. II, 463-78, published in a one-volume English edition as The Destruction of the Dutch Jews, New York, 1969. For the complete text of the interviews which Willy Lindwer conducted for his 1988 documentary "De Laatste Zeven Maanden: Vrouwen in het Spoor van Anne Frank" [The Last Seven Months: Women in the Footprints of Anne Frank], see the book (same title), Hilversum, 1988, published in English as The Last Seven Months of Anne Frank, New York, 1991. Among important studies on Bergen-Belsen are Sam E. Bloch, ed., Holocaust and Rebirth. Bergen Belsen 1945-1965, New York, 1965; Jo Reilly, David Cesarani, Tony Kushner and Colin Richmond, eds., Belsen in History and Memory, London, 1997, and Joanne Reilly, Belsen. The Liberation of a Concentration Camp, London, 1997; for a brief useful overview of the Belsen camp history compare also Shmuel Krakowski, "Bergen-Belsen," in Encyclopedia of the Holocaust, vol. 1, New York, 1990, 185-90.
8   AR 45/64: No. 395; Bauer, Ashes; "Belsen," in Konigseder/ Wetzel, Lebensmut, 173-218; Jozef Rosensaft, "Our Belsen", in Belsen, ed., Irgun Sheerit Hapleita Me'Haezor Habriti, Tel Aviv, 1957, 24-51; Jacob Trobe, oral communication, 9/24/1998.
9   Bauer, Ashes, 41.
10   Draft of letter from Jacob Trobe to Moses Leavitt, October 9, 1945, JDC NY Archives, Jacob Trobe collection. The letter was never

sent to Leavitt but was mailed at a later date to Adele Trobe

11   Jacob Trobe to Adele Trobe, letter 1 July 1945. Trobe has generously donated copies of the personal letters he wrote to his wife Adele while on assignment for the JDC (June 1944-January 1946) to the JDC NY Archives. See also Trobe letter undated, end of June, announcing his arrival in Belsen.

12   See also Angelika Konigseder and Juliane Wetzel, *Waiting for Hope: Jewish Displaced persons in Post-World War II Germany*, Evanston, 2001, p. 169 and Hagit Lavsky, *New Beginnings: Holocaust Survivors in Bergen-Belsen and the British Zone in Germany, 1945-1950*, Detroit, Michigan, 2002, pp. 59, 61.

13   Trobe letter, July 1, 1945.

14   Undated Trobe letter, early July 1945; Letter from Maurice Eigen, August 7, 1945, Report by Maurice Eigen, August 31, 1945, AR 45/64, file 395.

15   Undated Trobe letter, early July 1945.

16   Report by Maurice Eigen, letter from Eigen to Don (no last name), August 7, 1945, AR45/64, file 395.

17   Trobe letter, July 5, 1945.

18   Trobe letter July 6, 1945.

19   Trobe draft, October 9, 1945.

20   Trobe letter, July 5, 1945.

21   Trobe draft, October 9, 1945; Eigen report.

22   Interview with Norbert Wollheim, JDC NY Oral History Project, 1988.

23   Eigen report.

24   Trobe letters, September 3, September 7, and October 7, 1945; Eigen report; Eigen letter to Don, August 7, 1945. For more details on the activities of the JRU and its relations with JDC, see Lavsky, *New Beginnings*, and Joanne Reilly, *Belsen : The Liberation of a Concentration Camp*, Londen 1998, pp 118-144. See also the article by Thomas Rahe in this volume.

25   Trobe draft, October 9, 1945.

26   Eigen to Elliot Cohen, July 15, 1946, September 20, 1946, JDC NY Archives, AR45/64, file 395; David Wodlinger, "Report on the Activities of the JDC in the British Zone of Germany," JDC Jerusalem Archives, Geneva Collection, Box 487A, file Nr. Med. 32.

27   Trobe letter, September 18, 1945.

28   Dr. Nerson, Summary of the

Supplementary Report on Camp Bergen-Belsen, end September 1945; Report of Dr. Spanier, June 23, 1946; Harry Viteles, JDC and A.G. Brotman, JCRA (Jewish Committee for Relief Abroad, sponsored by the Central British Fund), "Survey on Conditions of Jews in the British Zone of Germany in March 1946," March 29, 1946, in JDC Jerusalem Archives, Geneva Collection, Box 491, file Nr. Med. 31. See also Report on Bergen-Belsen by Shlome Michael Gelber, June 28, 1946, AR45/64, file 395.

29   Trobe draft, October 9, 1945.

30   Joseph Rosensaft to Edward Warburg, November 17, 1945 and JDC cables October 3 and October 8, 1945, AR45/64 file 395; Trobe letter, September 11, 1945.

31   Trobe draft, October 9, 1945.

32   Rosensaft to Warburg, November 17, 1945.

33   Louis Sobel to Sam Jaffe, December 27, 1945, AR45/64, file 395.

34   Wodlinger report.

35   Translation of letter from Leib Kurland to the *Jewish Daily Forward*, May 6, 1946, AR45/64, file 395.

36   European Executive Council, Research Department, JDC Report no. 39, "JDC Activities in the British Zone of Germany, January-November 1947," (based on reports by Sam Dallob), JDC Jerusalem Archives, Geneva Collection, Box 487A, file Nr. Med. 32.

37   Viteles report, Trobe letter November 10, 1945. Also Lavsky, 144, 165, on the role of the British Chief Rabbi's Religious Emergency Council for European Jews in supplying kosher food.

38   Trobe letter, November 11, 1945.

39   Trobe letter, November 18, 1945.

40   Trobe letter, November 20, 1945.

41   Trobe letter, November 10, 1945. Also Trobe draft, October 9, 1945.

42   Wodlinger report.

43   Gelber report; Report no.39, 1947.

44   Gelber report; Report no.39, 1947.

45   Eigen to Warburg, May 20, 1946, AR45/64, 395.

46   Minna Levitas, "Memories – 1946-47", *Jewish Affairs*, (May

1979), pp. 27-30, JDC NY Archives; Wodlinger Report; Wodlinger to Eigen, May 2, 1946.

47   *AR 45/64: No. 395; Bloch, Holocaust and Rebirth; Bauer, Ashes; Alex Grobman, Rekindling the Flame. American Jewish Chaplains and the Survivors of European Jewry 1944-1948, Detroit, 1993.*

48   Wodlinger report; Report no. 39, 1947.

49   Gelber report.

50   Report no. 39, 1947.

51   *Idem.*

52   *Bloch, Holocaust and Rebirth; AR 45/64 No. 395; Idem No. 453: Germany, Organizations, Warburg Children's Home, Blankenese; Konigseder/Wetzel, Lebensmut, 188-94;* [*Yitzhak Tadmor, ed.*], *Duvdevanim al ha-elbah: Sippur Beit ha-yeladim be-Blankenese 1946-1948 (Cherries on the Elba. The Story of the Children's Home at Blankenese 1946-1948),* [Yad Yaari], *1996. I am indebted to Genya Markon for bringing me in contact with Sally Wideroff; Sally Wideroff, "First Legal Transport of Jews to Palestine," in Jewish Exponent, April 18, 1969, 2; telephone interview with Sally Wideroff, 6 October 1998; John Fink, written communication, November 1998; Madeleine Schulps, oral communication, November 16, 1998.*

53   Wodlinger Report; Markowitz to Eric Warburg, April 30, 1947, JDC Jerusalem Archives, Geneva Collection, Box 7A/2, file C48.403.

54   Report no. 39, 1947. Also Tadmor, ed., *Cherries on the Elba.*

55   Konigseder/Wetzel, *Waiting for Hope*, p. 195.

56   *Idem.* See also Gelber report; Report no. 39, 1947; Sam Dallob, Report for November 1947, JDC Jerusalem Archives, Geneva collection, Box 7A/1, file C48.009.

57   Rabbi Solomon Shapiro, Director for Religious Affairs, Reports for the months of October and November 1947 for the Religious Department, JDC NY Archives, AR45/64 file 406. See also Report no. 39, 1947.

58   See Viteles report.

59   The first JDC doctor in Belsen, Dr. Nerson , of OSE, established a home for expectant mothers in the British zone. See Gelber report, Report no. 39, 1947.

60   The Glyn Hughes hospital was named after Brigadier General H.L. Glyn Hughes, who directed the

medical rescue efforts of the British army in Bergen-Belsen immediately after the liberation of the camp. See correspondence and reports on Glyn Hughes in JDC Jerusalem Archives, Geneva collection, Box 491 and Box 272B.
61 Wodlinger report; Report no. 39, 1947.
62 See Sara Kadosh, "My Brother's Keeper: The American Jewish Joint Distribution Committee and the Brichah 1945-1948," in *Habricha: Escape and Flight from Europe to Eretz Israel 1945-1948*, eds., David Schiff and Asher Ben-Natan (Tel Aviv, 1998), pp. 20-24.
63 Wodlinger report.
64 Konigseder/Wetzel, *Waiting for Hope*, p. 43.
65 Herbert Katzki to Dr. William Schmidt, April 10, 1947, Dr. William Schmidt to Katzki, April 8, 1947, JDC Jerusalem Archives, Geneva collection, Box 7A/2 , file C48.410. See also Konigseder/Wetzel, *Waiting for Hope*, pp. 28, 51.
66 Lavsky, p. 207.
67 Report no. 39, 1947.
68 See Julie L. Kerssen, Life's Work: The Accidental Career of Laura Margolis Jarblum, M.A. thesis, University of Wisconsin – Milwaukee, 2000, p. 103. Also Bauer, *Ashes*, p. 243.
69 *Idem*. See also JDC Jerusalem Archives, Geneva collection, Box 22B, file S1405.
70 The 1948 U.S. Displaced Persons Act also opened the way for greater immigration to the U.S.

The task of remembering
1 The American Jewish Joint Distribution Committee, popularly known as "the Joint," was the major American agency aiding distressed Jews abroad. It provided welfare assistance to more than 130,000 European Jewish children, maintained in some 382 children's centers in postwar Europe. (Feature File story JDC press release, Raphael Levy, Publicity Director, 1947.)
2 Reminiscences by Betty Adler Rosenstock for proposed publication of the "Zippy Orlin" album.
3 Interview with Reuma Weizman, 1993, by Hagit Lavsky and Chana Kovari, The Oral History Division of the Institute of Contemporary Jewry, The Hebrew University, Jerusalem, 1993.
4 Ibid.

5 Letter from Rita Goldberg 2000
6 *Messages and Memories: Reflections on Child Survivors of the Holocaust*, Robert Krell, ed., second edition, p.100, Memory Press, Vancouver, BC., 2001
7 Elie Wiesel, *One Generation After*, Simon and Schuster, 1965.

"What it's really like in a D.P. Camp. A South African Girl In Belsen"
1 Bergen Belsen was not officially an extermination camp.
2 The burning of the barracks at Camp I began on April 24 and ended on May 21.

Exodus 47
1 Based in part on Aviva Halamish, *The Exodus Affair. Holocaust Survivors and the Struggle for Palestine* (London, 1998), Horst Siebecke: *Die Schicksalsfahrt der "Exodus 1947,"* Frankfurt am Main, 1987, Gunther Schwarzbergen, *Die letzte Fahrt der Exodus. Das Schiff das nicht ankommen sollte* (Göttingen, 1988, 1997).
2 The photographs appeared in various international newspapers and magazines. A selection of these photographs was also published in Sam E. Bloch (ed.), *Holocaust and Rebirth. Bergen-Belsen 1945-1965* (New York/Tel Aviv, 1965), pp. 181-187.
3 J.H. Fahlsbusch, S. Haake, F. Hurlin, P. Kononow, L. Krobitsch, *Pöppendorf statt Palästina, Zwangaufenthalt der Passagiere der "Exodus 1947" in Lübeck.* Publication issued for exhibition (Hamburg, 1999).
4 Josef Rosensaft at a press conference on September 4, 1947, *New York Herald Tribune*, European edition (Paris), September 5, 1947.
5 Ruth Gruber, *Exodus 1947. The Ship that Launched a Nation* (New York, 1999), pp. 181-185.
6 *New York Herald Tribune*, European edition (Paris), September 9, 1947.
7 Gunther Schwarzbergen, *Die letzte Fahrt der Exodus*, pp. 107-108.
8 *New York Herald Tribune*, European edition (Paris), September 10, 1947.
9 Interview Erik Somers and René Kok with Ursula Litzmann, Düren (Germany), Augustus 27, 2003.

10 As a freelance photographer, Ursula Litzmann sometimes sold copies of her photographs to individuals. Zippy Orlin probably purchased the photographs of the *Exodus* passengers from her and added them to her album.
11 In the Netherlands, for example on September 17, 1947 in *Nieuw Israëlitisch Weekblad*.
12 Sam E. Bloch (ed.), *Holocaust and Rebirth*, p. 184.
13 Aviva Halamish, *The Exodus Affair. Holocaust Survivors and the Struggle for Palestine* (London, 1998), pp. 226.
14 J.H. Fahlsbusch, *et al.*, *Pöppendorf statt Palästina*, chapters 17 and 19.
15 Noah Barou, "Remembering Belsen" in: *Belsen, Irgun Sheerit Hapleita Me'Haezor Habriti* (publ./ed.), (Tel Aviv, 1957), p. 85.
16 Aviva Halamish, *The Exodus Affair*, pp. 216-217, and Gunther Schwarzbergen, *Die letzte Fahrt der Exodus*, pp. 102-104.
17 Josef Rosensaft, "Our Belsen" in: *Belsen*, p. 46.
18 Noah Barou, "Remembering Belsen" in *Belsen*, pp. 85-86.
19 JDC 1947a. "Review of JDC Activity in the British Occupied Zone in Germany, January-November 1947" in Aviva Halamish, *The Exodus Affair*, p. 216.
20 J.H. Fahlsbusch, *et al.*, *Pöppendorf statt Palästina*, chapter 16.
21 *Ibid.*, chapter 19.
22 Angelika Königseder/Juliane Wetzel, *Lebensmut im Wartesaal. Die Jüdische DPs (Displaced Persons) im Nachkriegsdeutschland* (Frankfurt am Main, 1994), p. 211.
23 Hagit Lavsky, *New Beginnings. Holocaust Survivors in Bergen-Belsen and the British Zone in Germany, 1945-1950* (Detroit, 2002), p. 194.
24 Aviva Halamish, *The Exodus Affair*, p. 237.
25 J.H. Fahlsbusch, *et al.*, *Pöppendorf statt Palästina*, chapter 25.
26 Hagit Lavsky, *New Beginnings*, p. 196.

Authors

Sara Kadosh is Director of the American Jewish Joint Distribution Committee Archives in Jerusalem. She received her Ph.D. degree from Columbia University in 1995 and has been a Research Fellow at the International Institute for Holocaust Research at Yad Vashem. She remains affiliated with the Institute. Dr. Kadosh was Assistant Professor of Holocaust Studies at the graduate program of Touro College in Jerusalem, 2001-2002. Her articles on child rescue during the Holocaust, the post-war *Bricha* movement and Zionist history have appeared in academic journals and university publications. Dr. Kadosh is a contributor to *The Holocaust Encyclopedia*, ed. Walter Laqueur.

Angelika Königseder holds a Ph.D. in history and has been an academic staff member at the Center for Research on Anti-Semitism at the TU in Berlin. Her publications (with Juliane Wetzel) include *Lebensmut im Wartesaal. Die jüdischen DPs (Displaced Persons) im Nachkriegs-deutschland*, Frankfurt am Main, 1994 (English translation Evanston, 2001); *Flucht nach Berlin. Jüdische Displaced Persons 1945-1948*, Berlin, 1998, as well as several essays on the theme.

René Kok is a historian and head of the audio-visual archive at the Netherlands Institute for War Documentation in Amsterdam. He has written various articles and publications on photography and propaganda related to World War II: *Max Blokzijl. Stem van het Nationaal-Socialisme (Voice of the National-Socialism,* 1988), together with Erik Somers: *Het 40-45 Boek* (2002, featuring over 500 photographs from the NIOD archive.) *Naar Eer en Geweten. Gewone Nederlanders in een ongewone Tijd* (2001) and *V= Victory. Oorlogsaffiches 1940-1945* (2003, A study of posters in the Netherlands under the Nazi occupation). René Kok and Erik Somers edited the major reference work *Documentaire Nederland en de Tweede Wereldoorlog* (1989-1991).

Genya Markon obtained a B.S. from Skidmore College, spending her Junior Year at Hebrew University, Bezalel School of Art, Jerusalem, Israel. From 1981-1989 Genya Markon was Assistant Director of the Photo Services Department at the Israel Museum in Jerusalem. From 1989 to 1998 she was Director of Photo Archives at the U.S. Holocaust Memorial Museum. She is presently curator of Collections at the USHMM. Her chief publications are *Das Robinson Album: DP-Lager, Juden auf Deutschen Boden 1945-1948,* Jacqueline Giere and Rachel Salamander, article about the discovery of the album by Genya Markon. Christian Brandstatter, 1995, Vienna. *"History of Photography: Photography and the Holocaust"* Vol. 23, No. 4. Guest editors, Sybil Milton and Genya Markon, Winter 1999, Taylor and Francis, London, Philadelphia.

Eric Nooter (1950-2000) was a historian and obtained his Ph.D. in 1994 at the Free University of Amsterdam for his thesis entitled *Between Heaven and Earth: Church and Society in Pre-Revolutionary Flatbush, Long Island.* He was a specialist in Dutch colonial history and architecture and taught at several educational institutions. As a (guest) curator he designed a few exhibitions at leading international museums. From 1989 until his death in 2000, Eric Nooter was affiliated with the American Jewish Joint Distribution Committee in New York, most recently as Director of Archives & Records.

Thomas Rahe was awarded a Ph.D. in History and Catholic Theology at the Universität Münster in 1987. Since then he has been the academic director of the Bergen-Belsen memorial site; he has written several publications on Jewish history from the 19th and 20th centuries and on the social history of the Nazi concentration camps, including "Rabbiner im Konzentrationslager Bergen-Belsen," in *Menora 9* (1998), pp.121-152; *Häftlingszeichnungen aus dem Konzentrationslager Bergen-Belsen,* Hannover, 1993; "Höre Israel." *Jüdische Religiosität in nationalsozialistischen Konzentrationslagern,* Göttingen 1999.

Erik Somers is a historian at the Netherlands Institute for War Documentation. He has published articles and books about the history of World War II and has composed several exhibitions on the subject. His most recent publications: together with René Kok, *Het 40-45 Boek* (2002, featuring over 500 photographs from the NIOD archive), *Naar Eer en Geweten. Gewone Nederlanders in een ongewone Tijd* (2001) and *V= Victory. Oorlogsaffiches 1940-1945* (2003, A study of posters in Netherlands under the Nazi occupation). Together with Stance Rijpma, *Nederlanders, Japanners, Indonesiërs. Een opmerkelijke tentoonstelling* (2002, Dutch Japanese Indonesians, a remarkable exhibition). Erik Somers and René Kok edited the major reference work *Documentaire Nederland en de Tweede Wereldoorlog* (Dutch, 1989-1991).

Juliane Wetzel holds a Ph.D. in history. Since 1991 she has been an academic staff member of the Center for Research on Anti-Semitism at the TU Berlin. Her publications include *Jüdisches Leben in München 1945-1951. Durchgangsstation oderWiederaufbau?*, Munich, 1987; (with Angelika Königseder) *Lebensmut im Wartesaal. Die jüdischen DPs (Displaced Persons) im Nachkriegsdeutschland,* Frankfurt am Main 1994 (English translation Evanston, 2001); as well as several essays and reviews on the theme.

AMIDST
SINGING
AND
FEASTING
THE
CHILDREN
WERE
IMBUED
WITH
THE
MACCABEAN
SPIRIT.

SHALOM !

LEHITRAOT !

Colophon

This book is published with the assistance of a grant from the Stroum Book Fund, established through the generosity of Samuel and Althea Stroum.

editing
Phyllis Mitzman, Cambridge, Massachusetts

translation
Lee Mitzman, Amsterdam
The articles by Erik Somers and René Kok translated from Dutch.
The contributions from Angelika Königseder and Julia Wetzel and the article by Thomas Rahe translated from German.

design
Beukers Scholma and Inge van den Berg

sources
All photographs are from the photo album of Zippy Orlin (Netherlands Institute for War Documentation / NIOD), except for the photographs of the liberation of concentration camp Bergen-Belsen, p.16 through p.21 (NIOD).
p. 11, Hans Westerink, Zwolle
p.189 and p.190, Spaarnestad Fotoarchief, Haarlem, the Netherlands.
p.186, private collection Ursula Litzmann.

print
Waanders Printers, Zwolle

University of Washington Press
PO Box 50096
Seattle, WA 98145-5096, U.S.A.
www.washington.edu/uwpress

ISBN 0-295-98420-1

Netherlands Institute for War Documentation
Herengracht 380
1016 CJ Amsterdam
The Netherlands
info@niod..nl
www.niod.nl